The Hope
of the Christian

Otto Hentz, S.J.

A Michael Glazier Book
THE LITURGICAL PRESS
Collegeville, Minnesota

Zacchaeus Studies: Theology

General Editor: Monika Hellwig

A Michael Glazier Book published by The Liturgical Press

Cover design by David Manahan, O.S.B. Manuscript detail, "Christ in limbo," Der Landgrafenpsalter, 12th century.

1	2	3	4	5	6	7	8	9

Library of Congress Cataloging-in-Publication Data
Hentz, Otto J., 1938–
    The hope of the Christian / Otto Hentz.
       p. cm. — (Zacchaeus studies. Theology)
    "A Michael Glazier book."
    Includes bibliographical references.
    ISBN 0-8146-5860-1
    1. Future life—Catholic Church. 2. Immortality—Christianity. 3. Hope—Religious aspects—Christianity. 4. Catholic Church—Doctrines. I. Title. II. Series.
    BT902.H45   1997
    236'.2—dc21
                                        96-51703
                                            CIP

For
Martha Grogan Hentz

"Who lives in hope danceth without music"
(George Herbert, "Outlandish Sayings")

Acknowledgments

The basic work on this book was done while I was on sabbatical at the Weston School of Theology in Cambridge, Massachusetts. I would like to express thanks to the faculty and staff of Weston for their gracious hospitality and support. I would also like to express my gratitude to friends who read the text and made many helpful suggestions; in particular, William C. McFadden, S.J., and James Walsh, S.J., my colleagues in the theology faculty of Georgetown University.

Quotations from Scripture are taken from the Revised Standard Version.

Contents

Editor's Note on Zacchaeus Studies

This series of short texts in doctrinal subjects is designed to offer introductory volumes accessible to any educated reader. Dealing with the central topics of Christian faith, the authors have set out to explain the theological interpretation of these topics in a Catholic context without assuming a professional theological training on the part of the reader.

We who have worked on the series hope that these books will serve well in college theology classes where they can be used either as a series or as individual introductory presentations leading to a deeper exploration of a particular topic. We also hope that these books will be widely used and useful in adult study circles, continuing education and RENEW programs, and will be picked up by casual browsers in bookstores. We want to serve the needs of any who are trying to understand more thoroughly the meaning of the Catholic faith and its relevance to the changing circumstances of our times.

Each author has endeavored to present the biblical foundation, the traditional development, the official church position and the contemporary theological discussion of the doctrine or topic in hand. Controversial questions are discussed within the context of the established teaching and the accepted theological interpretation.

We undertook the series in response to increasing interest among educated Catholics in issues arising in the contemporary church, doctrines that raise new questions in a contemporary setting, and teachings that now call for wider and deeper appreciation. To such people we offer these volumes, hoping that reading them may be a satisfying and heartening experience.

Monika K. Hellwig
Series Editor

Introduction

A former student of mine spent his first year after college working for the poor in Peru. I had been to the rural town where he worked and knew his Peruvian "family." Reading his letters, I could picture the room his family set aside for him, picture the table where he wrote by candlelight. Ten years later, the opening paragraph of one letter still stands out for me:

> I started a letter twice last night, but just was not up to it. This morning I am determined. I think I know the root of my difficulty. The old saw has it, the cup is either half full or half empty, depending on how you look at it. My problem is, I have a full cup thirst.

What my friend wrote about his limitless desire and its present frustration articulates well the challenge to live in hope. He invites a Christian response, for Christians must be prepared to give an account for the hope that is in them (1 Pet 3:15). Such an account of our hope will set down what we are about as Christians, why it makes sense to us, and how we are to be about it. In giving an account of our hope, we will be proclaiming the gospel anew and letting our light shine for others.

Christians speak of three theological virtues: faith, hope, and love. About faith we speak at length: the unique kind of knowing that is faith, the motives for faith, and so on. And we speak at length of love: the nature of love, the difficulties of loving amid complex social forces, and so on. Surprisingly, though, we do not speak a great deal about hope.

True, we use the word hope frequently to introduce or qualify what we say. I hope your health improves. The negotiators hope to achieve a settlement. She hopes to do well in her exams. Such everyday talk tells us that hoping is a fundamental dynamic in our living. But when we speak of hope, we usually speak about what we hope for. We do not focus on the act of hoping. Although we sometimes ponder the challenges we face, we take for granted, as we move forward to meet them, the act of hoping that sustains our efforts.

The numerous changes we have had to face in recent times have made us acutely aware that we are historical beings, shaped by a past and summoned to shape a future. The challenges we confront call us beyond our individual or family living. Modern economic, social, political, and geopolitical problems make it clear that everything is interconnected. Looking to the future, we are tempted to ask: How can we be hopeful?

Perhaps it is not surprising that we speak so little about hoping. Hoping is so basic to life, like seeing or breathing, that we do not take notice of how it works in our lives until a crisis occurs (as when the lights go out or we are short of breath). As we shall see, in the dynamics of personal life hoping has a special place that makes it elusive, hard to define neatly. Moreover, there is a special poignancy in talk about hoping. Why? Simply put, hoping has to do with a deep yearning at the heart of us. It is easy to describe what we hope for, but each of our individual hopes is rooted in a more fundamental and all-embracing act of hoping. In the face of all the complexity, fragility, vulnerability, and frustration ingredient in our experience, hoping in this sense is the reach for what moves us at heart and defines our very being. That is why there is poignancy in talk about hoping: hoping defines our very being. To say there is no hope is to ring a death knell. Without hope there is no future for us, we have nothing to live for, life is pointless.

The subject of this volume is the hope of the Christian. Christians declare their ultimate hope in two words: eternal life. What does that expression mean? What is eternal life? We might answer in the following way: eternal life is the fullness of life in the kingdom of God, where the whole of redeemed humanity and our world, radically transformed in the immediate presence of God, have been brought to full and final perfection. But how does hope in eternal life relate to the challenges we face now? Does hope for eternal life devalue our world or distract us from responsibility for the world we shape? And what does it mean to say that we hope for eternal life? Why hope, precisely? What is hoping? Why do we hope in God? Does hope in God entail a demeaning dependency?

Anyone who wants to be a Christian in an intellectually honest way does not ponder those questions out of idle curiosity. Without hope in eternal life our future is, ultimately, only death, and death puts into question the meaning of life, of who we are now and what we are about in our history.

If an account of Christian hope is to be thoughtful, more than a reciting of catechetical formulas, we will have to explore fundamental issues, proceeding in stages.[1] We live in an age when we cannot take for granted the religious dimension of human experience. Our public culture is secular. When speaking of Christian life, we cannot presume that everyone accepts traditional doctrine and wants only fuller understanding and direction. We have to explain what we believe in a way that also explains why we can believe. We have to explain why being human means living in relation to God. Only then can we understand why talk of hope in eternal life does not amount to religious cant, why hoping in eternal life is central to authentic human living.

To understand Christian hope, then, we will first explore some fundamental topics: the freedom of the human person, the nature of hoping, hope in God, and the goal of our hoping, which is the promised kingdom of God. We will consider next the special problem of talking about the end time, something of which we have no direct experience.

The technical term for talk about the end time ("the last things") is eschatology, from two Greek words: *eschata,* last things, and *logos,* talk. Eschatology traditionally treats of the passage through death and resurrection to eternal life, the process of divine judgment, and the traditional notions of hell and purgatory.

After considering these topics, we will turn at last to an issue most critical to Christian hoping: the relation to eternal life of the shared history we are presently shaping in this world.

1

Freedom and Hope

One of my students had the habit of dropping by for a chat. I will never forget one of his visits. He just sat there for the longest time, staring at the floor. When he raised his head, there were tears in his eyes. This fellow was something special—good at his studies, an oarsman on the varsity crew, a resident assistant much admired by the first-year students for his thoughtfulness and the quiet intensity with which he moved through days quite full. But now the many problems in the world, an acute sense of responsibility, confusion about himself and about his future—all this, felt deeply, brought tears to his eyes. He at last broke the silence with this question: "Can I ever be happy?" We talked for a long while about how to find happiness amidst the complex challenges of life. The key to happiness, we finally decided, is love. And that, I would like to show, is what our hoping is all about.

Hoping is about the future. But the making of a future depends on human freedom. Because of our freedom human life is a story, a historical process by which we create a future. And the heart of the story is love—love of human persons and love of God. To examine the role of hoping in human life, then, we will explore two points: first, the relationship between hoping and freedom in creating a future; second, the central object of our hoping, the mystery of the person.[1]

Freedom, the Future, and Hoping

Personal life is not a matter of course. Persons do not move forward automatically, the way a machine runs. Nor do persons change simply by natural processes, as do plants or animals. Rather, persons live as persons by making choices. Hence, personal life is more than change. It is the making of a history, a choice-by-choice movement out of a past through the present into a future. True, some things apparently get settled. We find an agreeable job. We enter into a marriage partnership. But we settle into such engagements only by continually choosing them. We could change jobs. We could separate from our spouses. If we do stay with our engagements, we must choose whether to continue in the same style as before or adopt a new one. The future may be new because it is different in shape (through a change of jobs). Or the future may be new not in shape, but in style (working at the same job, but now as a veteran). But we live by choosing, by creating a future.

The future, though it does not yet exist, plays powerfully into the present. Our choices in the present make our future, so they depend on what we want for the future. In the present we must always look to the future. Otherwise, we would have no purpose. We would be spinning our wheels on a road to nowhere.

What moves us into a future is hoping. Hoping moves us to imagine possibilities. Once we envision possibilities we can make choices and move into a future. By hoping we reach out, look for, and embrace a vision and goals. And, on the basis of the vision we have embraced, hope impels us to live our lives in accordance with our vision and our goals.

No one will question that personal life means movement out of a past through a present into a future. Why, though, must we move into the future precisely by hoping? After all, we have minds. We can learn, reflect, and devise plans. We have wills. We can make choices, assert ourselves, create a future. And yet, analysis, planning, and commitment will suffice only for what we can manage on our own. When we cannot manage by ourselves, when we cannot by ourselves assure the future to which we look, we have to hope. Hoping is the reach for what is beyond our own capacity to calculate and control.

The future, in principle, is beyond our individual resources. We live within a natural environment that we cannot dominate. And we live within a complicated social context that we do not shape alone. That environment and social context challenge us to hope, to reach in freedom and try to shape in a shared history what certainly is beyond what we, on our own, can calculate and control.

The Nature and Necessity of Hope

For us to appreciate the nature and the necessity of hope, to appreciate that the future is simply beyond our calculus and control, we need only focus on the fact that our history is a history we share with other persons who are free. To understand hoping we have to understand what it means to share a history, to deal with the freedom of others. The heart of this process is loving. We now turn to the heart of the matter, love. Then we will be able to understand more fully the nature and necessity of hope.

Human persons come fully alive in love, when they are being loved, when they are loving. Though other things are more or less important (health, food, shelter, etc.), for true life nothing else, absolutely speaking, is necessary. Nothing else will supply its lack. Nothing else, however important or pleasureful, is at the center of life. Nothing else, if lost, means ultimate tragedy and death. Life at heart and center is life in love. To elaborate on our experience of love we can explore three important dimensions of love: creativity, gratuity, and solidarity.

Creativity

First, in the experience of being loved we come to appreciate love's creative power. The choice of another to love us brings us to life in a special way. To those who have known love there is no need to explain the joy, the peace, the vitality, the fulfillment in being loved. Perhaps nothing demonstrates the creative power of love better than forgiveness. When someone forgives us, it brings us, as it were, back to life. Further, when we know that we are loved, we know by that fact that we are loveable. Acceptance by another gives us self-confidence. That self-confidence, and the security of the other's love, empower us in turn to reach out to others in creative love.

Gratuity

Second, in the experience of life-giving love we come to understand gratuity. Why does someone love us? Love is unmerited, undeserved. We cannot make someone love us. We cannot make someone not love us. Love is a person's free choice. Love is gratuitous. It is the gift of another who chooses to accept us. Because love is free, it is beyond our calculus. We cannot exhaustively analyze another's free choice. Because love is free, it is beyond our willful control. We cannot manage another's freedom.

The gratuity of love makes it plain why we must relate to others in hope. Whatever our faith in others, we know them to be free. We have to hope in their choice to love us and in the steadfastness of their choice to love. To understand the necessity of hope, therefore, we need to examine the dynamics of choice.

Choice is not a blind, irrational act. Choice follows upon knowledge. The mind presents options perceived to have value. So choice is motivated, rational. But choice is not simply a matter of knowing. Persons are not computers. They do not respond to options automatically, through some purely rational calculus. Knowledge of options will yield only deliberation. Different persons, faced with the same options, make different choices. So we cannot reduce an act of choice to an act of the mind, to knowledge and deliberation. The will is involved. We have to choose how we will evaluate the options, how we will be rational. In other words, in the act of choice there is an interaction of mind and will. The mind interacts with the will, presenting options for choice; the will interacts with the mind, choosing how it will respond to the options. The two cannot be divorced. Otherwise, choice would be mindless, irrational; it would not be free, but automatic, impersonal. Mind influences will and will influences mind. What we know limits the choice of who we can will to be, but who we choose to be affects the way we use our knowledge.

The mutual interaction of mind and will in free choice explains why we cannot exhaustively analyze or calculate a free choice. Though a personal choice is motivated and rational, we choose how we will be rational.[2] Therein lies the originality in choice.

This originality in freedom constitutes the mystery of the person. Because of their freedom and originality, persons have a richness and depth that make them incalculable and mysterious. The mystery has nothing to do with a lack of rationality in persons or a weakness in our ability to "figure out" someone. Persons are intelligible, but because they are free they have a different kind of intelligibility than things. It is not really possible to know what makes a person tick. We cannot plot persons the way we can chart the circuitry of an electrical appliance. Who a person is, is who a person chooses to be, and that is beyond our calculus and control. No wonder we revere loyalty and fidelity. We know that the response of other persons is free. We have to live in hope of their love.

Solidarity

Third, in the experience of love we come to understand, along with creativity and gratuity, human solidarity. For, in the experience of love, one understands that freedom is interpersonal, oriented to solidarity with others. To explain that fact, the most important fact about human life, requires two simple steps: first, freedom has a specific orientation; second, the most important object of freedom is other persons.

Freedom is not a neutral mechanism. Freedom has a specific orientation. The proper object of freedom is what is good. Had freedom no specific orientation, we would not distinguish right from wrong. We could not use our freedom badly, or for that matter use it well. We tend to evaluate human choices by some quality like lucidity or consistency, but not by their content, by the object intended. Authentic freedom, however, is not simply choosing, but choosing the good. The experience of love proves the point. Freedom is for love. The loss of a loved one puts the lie to a notion of freedom as simply a neutral capacity for choice that has no specific orientation.

Second, the most important good we choose is other persons. Of course, this point is basic to a Christian understanding of human life. But Jesus' command that we love one another is not arbitrarily imposed. In the experience of love we come to understand the most important object of our freedom, namely, other persons to be accepted and brought to life by love. Freedom, then, is social essentially, of its nature, in its very purpose and meaning as freedom.

There is a serious challenge in the realization that we move into a future only by relating to others, only by hoping with, hoping in, others. What of our independence and unique individuality? Does the freedom of others put us in competition with them and compromise our own freedom? To reply to this challenge we need to ask ourselves: Does love bring us to life and liberate us, or does it compromise our freedom, constrict us, deaden us? Those who have experienced love know that we are free not despite the freedom of others, but precisely in relation to their freedom. If our freedom is essentially social, then to adjust freely to others for the sake of a common good, for the sake of communion, does not compromise our freedom. Our unique individuality finds fulfillment precisely in and through communion with others.

In order to move into a future, we need the help of others. Because we reach in hope for what is beyond our individual resources, hoping is always hoping in others. Further, hoping is always hoping *with* others because we need their support to maintain our belief and sustain our commitment with courage and perseverance. We need, in various ways, the support of family, friends, colleagues, fellow citizens. Not least, we need the support of the community of Christian faith. It follows that solidarity in hope means more than the support we look to receive from others. Human solidarity means as well the support we are called to provide for others. We need to appreciate our ability to enliven their hope by hoping in and with them.

Shortly, we shall consider hoping as, first and last, hoping in God. First, we turn to a consideration of the dynamics of hoping.

2

Hoping

A few years ago, a seminarian preparing to work in Africa became a regular member of my Wednesday night student discussion group. On his last night with us he asked the students if they would be willing to answer a personal question.

"When I was younger," he said, "about your age, I had a dream. I still have my dream. You and I have become friends. Tell me, what is your dream?"

The response? Silence. In the end no one answered his question. The conversation turned to other matters. Perhaps the question caught them off guard because it was so direct, perhaps it was a question they had never thought to ask themselves, or perhaps they knew very well what their dream was but were shy about revealing something so deeply personal. The seminarian's question addresses what moves us at heart, our basic vision and goals, our hoping. We turn now to a consideration of what it is to hope.

We can begin with a definition of hoping. Hoping is the reach of the human person for a future that is possible, desired, but beyond the person's ability to achieve it. The reach of hope, unlike mere wishing, is at the heart of personal life. It is a reach for what defines our very selves. Thus, hoping is an active reach by which we move into our future with courage and perseverance.

Faith, Hope, and Love

To understand the dynamics of hope it helps to situate the act of hope within the familiar trinity of faith, hope, and love.

Somehow these three virtues are distinct, otherwise we would not bother to name three. Somehow the three are interconnected, for the life of a human person, though a complex process, is one life. Actually, faith and hope and love are so intimately interconnected that we often use the words in a way that makes their distinctive meanings overlap. Sometimes, for example, faith designates not just a way of knowing, but a trust that is as much love and hope as it is faith. And yet, the three words are not interchangeable terms. They designate movements of the human spirit that are distinct from one another, but intimately related. To explore the intimate relationship of faith, hope, and love, marriage provides a good model.

Think of a woman and man about to make their wedding vows. How did their wedding love come to pass? How did this woman and man meet, get to know one another, and grow in their love? Their story could be described as a dance of hoping and believing and loving. At the beginning, the two were needful, open, on the look, reaching out. They reached out to one another. That reaching is hoping. And because they reached out, they took notice of one another, got a first appreciation of one another, came to know one another. That knowing is faith. And because they came to know one another, they reached out, in a further movement of hope, to affirm and accept one another. That acceptance is love. Had there not been at work in them some reach, some stretching beyond themselves, they would not have gotten to know one another. Then, had there not been at work in them some further hope, they would not have reached out to accept one another in love.

The process is a vital interaction of reaching in hope, knowing in faith, and accepting in love. Because they stretched beyond themselves (hope), they came to know one another (faith). But they needed to act on what they knew of one another in faith in order to reach out on the basis of what they knew (hope). And because, on the basis of their faith, they reached out in hope, they not only imagined a relationship, they made it real by accepting one another (love). Their love empowered them to reach out anew in hope, and so to know one another afresh in faith. Knowing one another more deeply they reached out anew in hope, so as to be more deeply together in love. It is the most beautiful dance: the dance of hoping-believing/hoping-loving/hoping-believing. It is the dance of three, each of which makes possible the movement of the others, summoning, supporting, and completing one another. Indeed, as our hoping dances to deeper faith and love, it becomes more confident, more trusting.

The classic formula (faith, hope, love) locates hope as the "medium" of faith and love. Hope moves us to faith and then, finding its support in faith, hope moves us to love. Hope moves us to love and love leads to deeper faith. Hoping is the fundamental act out of which faith and love arise, and they in turn foster its growing power. Hope, then, is the central dynamic of the human spirit, its power of reach.

The Experience of Hope

We may gain a more precise understanding of the act of hoping by considering the kind of things we hope for, the qualities ingredient in hoping, and the profoundly personal character of hoping.

First, hoping is about something serious. We all indulge in wishful thinking. But we do not cultivate anticipation about such wishes because we know them to be fantasies and dismiss them readily. We certainly do not confuse them with what we truly hope. No, we hope for what is important to us. That accounts for a certain poignancy in talk about our hope. Our hoping expresses a real need or deep yearning that relates to our very being. To put the point another way, we do not despair when disappointed in unimportant matters. To hope for rain to end a drought is one thing; to wish for sun merely to get a deeper tan is another. True hoping does not engage trivial matters.

Second, hoping is about something possible, something that we can realistically envision. Otherwise, we would be focusing on a fantasy not rooted in concrete experience, not rooted in real possibilities. Because the object of hoping is something serious and possible, yet not automatically assured, we distinguish hoping from the wishful thinking born of immaturity or ignorance. In hoping, unlike wishing, we imagine that what we hope for can and will come to pass.

Third, hoping is about something that is open to question. We do not have to hope for what is inevitable or assured. We have only to expect it. Hoping, unlike expecting, imagines something to be possible that is not inevitable, something which from the look of things may even be dubious. The point here is not about the difficulty in getting what we want. Unloading a truck might be difficult, but we know that we can do it, given time and effort. When we lack this kind of assurance, when we have no such guarantee, we may still hope.

Next, let us consider several qualities at work in our hoping. Will the newborn be healthy? Will the peace negotiations yield a settlement? Will a friend forgive me? In the end, will God find in me faith that is genuine? Faced with such questions, hoping requires more than patience. Hoping requires courage. We need courage to reach for something that is serious, yet uncertain. A second quality at work in hoping is perseverance. A reach for what is serious but not assured means our hope must be steady and constant. Perseverance is simply courage operative through extended time (as fidelity is simply love operative over time).

We might further characterize hoping as confident anticipation. Hoping is an active anticipation. Indeed, our active anticipation turns what might be possible into what is plausible. For by our hoping we dispose ourselves to work at what shows promise for the future. In the active anticipation of hope there is a certain confidence that does not shrink before uncertainty. Radical doubt or cynicism undercuts the courage and perseverance that sustain genuine hope. Loss of all confidence means an end of hoping. If we do not muster the courage and perseverance that are part of hoping, we reduce the hope at the heart of us to empty wishing. The face of hope is not always sunny and cheerful. It might be anxious or deeply troubled. Indeed, in the liturgy we pray, "keep us free from anxiety as we wait in joyful hope." But confidence yields a sense that perseverance is right, and with that a certain centeredness and peace. This peace may not be blissful or serene, but in hoping there is somehow a vital peace we cannot otherwise enjoy.

Finally, let us speak of the profoundly personal character of hoping. Our hoping is of our choosing. In hoping, we do not dream or wish. We do not wait for what will one day surely arrive. In hoping, we act. Because we reach for what is not assured, our hoping is a quite personal choice. In our hoping, we choose and define ourselves. An act of courage may serve as a dramatic example. A person plunges into turbulent waters to rescue someone from drowning. Such an act of courage puts that person on the line, defines the person. In the same way, hoping involves our deepest subjectivity. In our hoping, we commit ourselves.

The subjectivity in hoping points to the incalculable richness of human experience. The necessity of living in hope does not derive from personal inadequacy in mind or will. Rather, the object of hope, our future, is such as to require the subjectivity in our hoping. On the one hand, hope reaches for what is beyond individual control. On the other hand, in hoping we shape ourselves and our shared history with the creativity and originality of our own freedom. The alternative would be a life that is automatic, impersonal, inhuman.

To further clarify the nature of hope and the intense subjectivity in hoping, it helps to consider the dispositions contrary to hoping: presumption and despair.

Presumption and Despair

Presumption and despair are contrary reactions to the one basic challenge in hoping, namely, accepting the fact that the future is beyond our calculus and control. A presumptuous person is happily certain of the exact shape of the future. A despairing person is unhappily certain that a hoped-for future will never arrive. Both the presumptuous and the despairing map the realm of the possible according to their personal calculations.

Presumption is an error, but every error contains a truth. The truth in presumption is that, yes, God will inevitably fulfill the promises made to us. When presumptuous, however, we forget that God, precisely as love, acts gratuitously, in a manner beyond our mastery. Of course, everyday life readily gives the lie to the naive self-assertion of presumption. In the school of experience we learn the lesson of how to hope in God.

The more common alternative to authentic hoping is despair. Despair is a dramatic term. We think of a person in despair as someone who has given up. The heart has gone out of life. To live is to see possibility, and so to have a future, and so to have a meaningful present. A person in despair cannot imagine any possibilities. There seems to be no way out, no place to go, no possibilities for movement or improvement. Hoping moves us to imagine possibilities. Without hoping, without imagining possibilities, how can there be any meaningful yearning, anything to live for?

But perhaps the situation is not simply one of tragic deadlock. There may be more going on than we at first perceive. Despair might actually signal a certain vitality. The despairing person, however profoundly frustrated and confused, at least engages life, not content to "hunker down" in resignation. A comparison of hope and despair with love and hatred makes the point. It is a commonplace that the opposite of love is not hatred, but indifference. Hatred at least takes seriously, engages, the object of hate. Indifference, on the other hand, looks away, pays no attention. In the same way, the true opposite of hope is not despair, but cynicism and apathy. Despair engages us at heart. It implies a yearning, a reach, an urge, a pressure. And the reach is not for something fantastic, but something dimly felt to be really possible. The cynical and apathetic, on the other hand, presuppose that not much is possible. They are the ones who are truly trapped. They give up on the hoping that impels us to imagine possibilities and thereby opens up a future, however obscure. Without hope there will be no future, no commitment, no vitality, no authentically human life.

The problem with all we have said so far about hoping is that it might seem too tidy. Distinctions, comparisons, and definitions might clarify the notion of hope. At stake, however, is not a notion, but the dynamic reach at the heart of life. A person lives out of a basic spirit, a fundamental reach to know and act, and so to create a future. To explore the basic orientation and reach of the human spirit we turn to our relationship with the mystery of God. For, first and last, our hope is hope in God, the hope that grounds, embraces, and enlivens all hoping.

3

Hope in God

One night a group of priests was enjoying an evening together. We were all seasoned veterans of the upheavals in the Church during the 60s, accustomed to rethinking everything we had been taught to see if it still made sense. One of our group said he had been asked to preside at a wedding where neither party would accept the idea of having children. Did we think that was a valid marriage? The obvious answer was no, at least according to the old definition of marriage, but we began to test the idea, to think of various ways it might be valid. Then he told us their reason: the world was such a sorry place that they did not want to bring children into it. Suddenly, we had unanimity. Everyone began to say there was a serious problem there. In my view, such a marriage is hopeless. How can you celebrate a Christian wedding when the bride and groom have so little hope in God that they have no hope for our world?

Hope in God: these words might seem inappropriate to some or facile to others. Inappropriate, because talk of God sounds bizarre in our secular culture, out of place in the real world of everyday affairs, of import only for private moments of piety. Or facile, for how is it possible to sustain hope in God, given the confusions and suffering in our world?

For the Christian, however, at the heart of all hoping is hope in God. Why? For the Christian, to be human means to be, at heart and center, in relationship to God. Our relationship to God is the context of all that we are, of all that we do. God is not one being alongside other beings, whom we are free to deal with or ignore. God is the Creator and Lord of all, inescapable, all-embracing. We who are made in the image and likeness of God are by that fact called to a personal relationship with God.

Human hoping exemplifies the fundamental relationship with God that defines all human endeavor. We hope for a lot of things. Often our hopes do not come to pass. Still, we go on hoping. We spontaneously distinguish particular hopes from hoping. This suggests that our hoping is directed at something deeper than particular hopes. Particular hopes have only relative value. Relative to what? What is it that is of ultimate value for us? What do we use to measure the depth and breadth, the reach of the human heart? The mystery of God. In comparison with God, all other things have only limited value—true value, but limited. Ultimately, the goal of human yearning lies in union with God. All our particular hopes are manifestations of our fundamental, all-encompassing hope in God.

A simple analogy might clarify this all-embracing quality of our hope in God. We can engage in a variety of physical exercises, such as jogging or swimming, because we have the basic capacity to exercise. But it is not because we can swim or jog that we have the basic capacity to exercise. Rather, it is because we first have a basic capacity for exercise that we can do the particular exercises of swimming and jogging. At work in all our exercise is a basic capacity that is not limited to this or that particular exercise. Similarly, a basic capacity underlies the whole of human activity. Created in the image and likeness of God, summoned by our very nature to union with God, the human spirit is a dynamic capacity for the infinite. Our reach for the infinite, therefore, is not a particular activity alongside other human activities. The reach for the infinite is at work in all human activities, each of which is a limited expression of the deepest reach of the human spirit, the reach to God.

What most poignantly reveals the hope at the heart of life is the limitation we feel in all our experience. Not only when our hopes are frustrated, but even in our most satisfying moments, we are always aware of limitation. In fact, we know that each one of our experiences is only a passing moment in a life story, which itself is but one among countless stories in human history. To live, to take seriously our experience in the world, is to hope that our lives culminate in a unity that draws the fragmentary moments of our experience together with the lives of others with whom we share a common history.

It is because the human spirit is a boundless capacity measured only by the mystery of God that in everything apart from God we experience limitation and must live in hope. The hope at the heart of life is hope in God as the ultimate one who embraces our history in self-giving love. God, the Creator, can draw all things together in unity. God can guarantee the ultimate meaning of human life in the world by allowing our lives together to share in the infinite life of God.[1]

The Necessity of Hope

God's self-giving love is altogether beyond our control, so we can relate to God only in hope. If, in the case of all other persons, we must relate to them in hope because their free response to us eludes our power, this must be true in the highest degree with respect to God.

But hoping in God does not go unchallenged. If God is the goal of our hoping, what sustains our hoping now in the face of suffering and evil? Again and again, out of the pain people experience, the question arises: Why? Again and again, only this becomes clear: The question has no logical answer. The explanations we have heard ("We suffer because of our sins" or "Suffering teaches us lessons we need to learn") are never finally, fully satisfying. The fact is that "the problem of evil utterly defeats philosophy."[2] The philosopher wants to explain the meaning of things, but evil does not make sense. One cannot make sense of the nonsensical, explain the inexplicable.

But Christians hope. What do Christians know of God that motivates and sustains their hoping? Is their hoping merely childish wishing or a desperate projection of an illusory savior? No, Christians pray: "Out of the depths I cry to you, O Lord" (Ps 130:1). They pray out of a poverty that directs them to where, ultimately, their deepest resources lie. They reach out in hope to the mystery of God and find in faith God's self-gift, God's self-revelation in Christ.

Revelation in Christ

What a remarkable gift, revelation. If persons choose not to reveal themselves, we can relate to them only by guessing about them, projecting some image on them. But if persons do reveal themselves, then we know them as they really are. With the gift of revelation we know them to be of this or that quality, standing toward us in this or that way. Of course, this does not mean they become fixed in this one posture and lose their freedom and creativity. But, so far as their self-revelation is true, so far do we know, by their own account, who they choose to be, how they choose to stand toward us.

This can help us to better grasp the mystery of God. Although Christians speak of Jesus Christ as a specific historical figure, when they use the word God they sometimes seem to imagine a faceless, undefined being. But for Christian faith God is not God-in-general, but the Father of Jesus Christ. God's own gracious Word tells us how we are to understand God, how God in sovereign freedom actually stands toward us, and why finally we can hope in God.

When the mystery of God first reveals itself to Israel we learn that God is compassionate love. God tells Moses, "I know their sufferings" (Exod 3:7). When God speaks through the prophets, we hear again and again of God's compassion. And when the history of revelation culminates in the life, death, and resurrection of Christ, we have the decisive revelation of the steadfast, compassionate love of God. To Jesus' ultimate prayer of hope, "Father, into thy hands I commit my spirit!" (Luke 23:46), the response is that God raises him to new life. And so, the Christian proclaims with Saint Paul:

> If God is for us, who is against us? He who did not spare his own Son but gave him up for us all, will he not also give us all things with him? For I am sure that neither death, nor life, . . .

nor anything else in all creation, will be able to separate us from the love of God in Christ Jesus our Lord (Rom 8:31-32, 38-39).

The compassionate, steadfast love of God decisively revealed in Christ is what founds and sustains Christian hoping.

In Jesus Christ we learn that the mystery of God has chosen to be God-with-us. That is who the mystery of God is: God-with-us. What a wonderful revelation about ourselves and the history that we share and shape. Our story is God's own story. We are not merely creatures of God. We are summoned to personal union with God, for we are "fellow heirs with Christ" (Rom 8:17), who is "the first-born among many brethren" (Rom 8:29), "the pioneer and perfecter of our faith" (Heb 12:2). To see what this means for Christian hoping we need to look at the man Jesus, to reflect on the story of Jesus as told in the New Testament.

God's self-revelation in Christ is not an idea, but the concrete person, life, and destiny of Jesus. Jesus is not "everyman." He is an individual man with a specific history. He was called to a particular mission in which he enjoyed some success but created powerful enemies. One spring day he was crucified on a hill outside Jerusalem. Jesus lived in a certain way because of what he understood about God's love, about who God wills to be for us and who God wills that we be for one another and for God. Jesus is, therefore, the source and the model of Christian hoping.

What did Jesus hope for? The kingdom of God. Jesus' vision of the kingdom shaped the whole of his ministry: "The time is fulfilled, and the kingdom of God is at hand" (Mark 1:15). Jesus signaled the inauguration of the kingdom with deeds of healing, forgiveness, and solidarity with the oppressed. But the kingdom is God's future with us, God's to accomplish, in God's time.

Why did Jesus live and work in hope? The basis of Jesus' hope was his relationship with the Father. Jesus taught in sermons and parables what the Father meant to him. In his work Jesus also teaches us about the Father, for the son does the Father's will, reveals the Father's love, and promotes the reign of God which embodies that love.

Nothing tells us better how God "thinks future" than Jesus' teaching of forgiveness in word and deed. Forgiveness gives us a future by releasing us from our sin and thereby redeeming our past. Jesus expresses his understanding of God's compassionate love in the moving parable of the prodigal son. A father welcomes home a son who was lost to him. The father does not even bother to listen to the son's carefully rehearsed act of contrition. Indeed, "while he was yet at a distance, his father saw him and had compassion" (Luke 15:20).

How Jesus hoped we know from the whole course of his life and ministry. He compared the gradual coming of the kingdom to the growth of a mustard seed or the action of yeast in dough. And yet, he knew that his message presented a radical challenge to his listeners. He sensed that the kingdom's growth would encounter the same misunderstanding and opposition that he himself did. This awareness may be seen in his parables about the seed that failed to take root or about the enemy who sowed cockle in a farmer's wheat field.

Nonetheless, Jesus' hope did not waver. He pursued his mission with zeal, for his hoping was rooted in his understanding of God: "With God all things are possible" (Matt 19:26). His deepest lesson in hope was his surrender to the Father's will: "If it be possible let this cup pass from me; nevertheless, not as I will, but as thou wilt" (Matt 26:39). He fulfilled that surrender on the cross: "Father, into thy hands I commit my spirit!" (Luke 23:46).

Resurrection and Eternal Life

The history of Jesus culminates in his resurrection. What does the resurrection tell us about Jesus, about God, and about ourselves?

ABOUT JESUS

The resurrection proclaims God's definitive acceptance of Jesus' person and of Jesus' life of obedient service in fidelity to his mission. In their experience of the risen Christ his disciples fully realize Jesus' unique relationship with the Father and the uniquely salvific meaning of Jesus' person, ministry, and death. His life of self-giving love culminates in eternal life. Paul puts the matter clearly: "He humbled himself and became obedient unto death. . . . Therefore God has highly exalted him" (Phil 2:8-9).

ABOUT GOD

The resurrection manifests God's steadfast love. Out of self-giving love the faithful God calls us to eternal life. God is "not God of the dead, but of the living" (Matt 22:32).

ABOUT OURSELVES

The resurrection confirms that we are called to eternal union with God. In Jesus' resurrection God inaugurates the fullness of the kingdom. This Jesus who was raised is said to be the head of the body (Col 1:18), the cornerstone of a holy temple (Eph 2:20), the vine that gives life to many branches (John 15:5), the firstborn of many children (Rom 8:29). The person and life and victory of Christ are not for Christ's sake, but, as the Creed proclaims, "for us and for our salvation."

We learn from the resurrection that there is no *next* world, *next* life. God redeems *this* life, *this* world for fulfillment in the kingdom: "For God sent the Son into the world, not to condemn the world, but that the world might be saved through him" (John 3:17). It is precisely because God shares divine life with us now that we have as our ultimate future a fulfillment of our history in the kingdom of God.

The resurrection announces God's decisive response to human suffering and death. In the reality of Jesus, God's own human reality, God radically identifies with human suffering and death. Jesus' prayer during his agony, "If it be possible, let this cup pass from me" (Matt 26:39), did not forestall the crucifixion. God "did not spare his own son" (Rom 8:32). But God reveals in the resurrection that suffering will not be without vindication. There is no explanation here, no theological theory. The response to the problem of suffering is not on the level of theory, but on the level of action. The resurrection reveals that what God did to alleviate suffering during the earthly ministry of Jesus was only an anticipation of the end time, when God "will wipe away every tear" (Rev 21:4).

God's revelation in Christ tells who we truly are. It makes clear what the history we make in this world is all about, for it speaks of the future to which we are called. That future, of course, puts to us an elemental, soul-shaking question. The toughest problem for Christian faith might be not the reality of God, and not the reality of God-made-human in the person of Jesus, but our own reality. Is our life of such depth and import that God's very Spirit is at work enlightening, strengthening, and sanctifying us? Given what we know of the human from ourselves, it can be hard to believe in God becoming human. A look into a mirror, a casual glance at any newspaper must give us pause. Is it with us that God has chosen to be? Yes. The Creed is clear: "for us and for our salvation." The mystery of God, by its own free choice, has become God-with-us. It is not merely a possibility. It is not an intention. It is a fact. It is a fact that defines the very being of God. It is a fact that defines our being, our history. God loves us personally. God calls us to life and sustains us out of love. God shares with us divine life and love. God's love is steadfast, forgiving again and again. God summons us to fullness of life and love in the kingdom. That is the good news. That news sustains our hoping.

4

The Kingdom of God

The dominant metaphor for the ultimate goal of Christian hope is the kingdom of God.[1] The coming of God's reign was the focus of Jesus' mission: "Now after John was arrested, Jesus came to Galilee, preaching the gospel of God, and saying, 'The time is fulfilled, and the kingdom of God is at hand; repent, and believe in the gospel'" (Mark 1:14-15).

The Old Testament

The notion of the reign of God has its origin in the tradition of Israel. That tradition shaped the religious imagination of Jesus and the people Jesus addressed. To appreciate the vision that guided Jesus' mission we need to review the development of Israel's hope in the reign of God.

Revelation comes to us in our history. Our relationships—whether as children, friends, spouses, parents, or as persons of faith in God—undergo constant development as we confront change and challenge, disappointment or success, or simply surprise, in our history. We have constantly to renew our faith and refine our hope. Otherwise, we would lose the basis on which we live now and for the future. In the same way, Israel developed its hope for fulfillment through a continuous rethinking of its history in light of God's promise. Hence, the "kingdom of God" is a metaphor that embraces a rich set of ideas developed over a long period of time.

KINGSHIP AND PROMISE

A specific historical experience shaped the faith of Israel. God intervened in history to liberate the people from enslavement in Egypt. Their liberation revealed that God is the Lord of history. Then, through the covenant at Sinai, Israel became a people of the promise, a people with a future, a people of hope.

A sense of destiny inevitably leads to reflection on beginnings. The thought of a future, where it will all end, leads to thoughts of the past, how it all began. Thus, prophetic reflection on the Exodus and the covenant at Sinai leads to the insight that the Lord of history is indeed the Creator of the universe. If God rules the world and calls history to a specific destiny, then God must be the Creator who first established the world with a view to a specific goal. The Lord is king of the whole created world:

> The earth is the LORD's and the fulness thereof,
>   the world and those who dwell therein.
> Who is this King of glory?
>   The LORD of hosts,
> he is the King of glory! (Ps 24:1, 10).

What thwarts the divine plan is human sin. Sin alienates persons from God, from one another, from nature, as is shown in the inspired story of the fall in Genesis, which narrates the consequences of sin for society and its future. Muddied waters have effect all around and downstream. First, Adam sins, then Cain murders his brother, and things continue to deteriorate until the purifying flood overwhelms the original creation gone bad. But God is faithful and establishes a series of covenants with Noah, with Abraham, and with Moses at Sinai.

Suffering and frustration tested and purified Israel's trust in God. Though Israel believed itself to be a nation to whom God had promised land and prosperity, their actual experience was of continual insecurity. Again and again, Israel had to renew and redefine its hope in the kingdom of God. Their hope had its basis in the covenantal promise of God, who is Creator of the world and sovereign Lord of history. Israel had experienced the Lord's sovereignty in its own history: deliverance from Egypt, direction in the wilderness, the covenant at Sinai, the Promised Land, defense against enemies. The canticle of Moses celebrates these works of God and concludes, "The LORD will reign for ever and ever" (Exod 15:18). Israel lived in hope, for it remembered God's fidelity. Hence, their classic creed:

> A wandering Aramean was my father; and he went down into Egypt. . . . And the Egyptians treated us harshly. . . . Then we cried to the LORD the God of our fathers, and the LORD heard our voice, and saw our affliction; . . . and the LORD brought us out of Egypt. . . . He brought us into this place and gave us this land, a land flowing with milk and honey (Deut 26:5-9).

In the first stages of religious development Israel hopes for a fulfillment that is quite concrete and focused. It does not embrace humankind in general, nor does it look to a life beyond death in a heavenly realm. Salvation will be a state of affairs in this world: a people secure in their identity and in their land, enjoying peace and prosperity and the prospect of numerous progeny. These material blessings will result when God reigns, that is, when God is fully effective in the lives of the nation, when the people live according to God's will, in accordance with the covenant. Reverence for God, compassion and care for one another, especially those in need—that is the set of relationships which is right and just. When God reigns, there is justice. When there is justice, there is security, peace, and prosperity. Although metaphors other than king are used (shepherd, father, redeemer, mother, warrior), the notion of divine sovereignty is a constant.

The Lord works through human instruments. At first, the leaders were judges, men called in times of crisis for a special role. Eventually, a monarchy was established under King David. It is with the institution of a monarchy that the sovereignty of God takes on the specific designation of kingship. King David will be the instrument through which Yahweh, the sovereign Lord, will accomplish the fulfillment for which Israel hopes.

Israel's worship celebrates the many dimensions of the Lord's kingship: God as Creator, God as Savior of Israel, God as Lord of all the earth, all nations. To cite one psalm:

> Clap your hands, all peoples!
> Shout to God with loud songs of joy!
> For the LORD, the Most High, is terrible,
> a great king over all the earth.
> He subdued peoples under us,
> and nations under our feet (Ps 47:1-3).

Because Israelite faith looks to an end, an eschaton, in which the fulfillment of their history will be achieved, it may be called an eschatological faith. There are two overlapping phases in the development of their understanding of what salvation will mean: prophetic eschatology and apocalyptic eschatology.

PROPHETIC ESCHATOLOGY

The first phase is prophetic eschatology. Prophecy is not about a crystal-ball prediction of the future, but a matter of political realism. Because God exercises sovereignty by acting in history, prophets interpret history, so to interpret God's will for the nation and articulate a hope for future fulfillment.

Prophetic eschatology looks for God to establish a kingdom within history through a human instrument, a Messiah, an anointed king. As a people under God's rule, Israel will prosper. At first, the prophets emphasize judgment, the day of the Lord, when the people will be called to account for their godless ways. But the prophets leave the people with reason for hope, and, in time, they emphasize the promise of redemption.

Prophetic eschatology develops through three stages. At first, hope looks to the Davidic dynasty. God empowers the king, whom Yahweh addresses as "my son" (Ps 2:7). The prophets emphasize the power and influence of God. The king is to act in the compassionate manner of God, serving justice and attending to the poor. Through David God will establish an everlasting reign. In fact, however, the Davidic kingdom is divided: the northern kingdom is conquered by Assyria and the southern kingdom falls to Babylon. The prophets interpret these disasters as a judgment on a people unfaithful to the covenant.

After David's dynasty collapses, there is a second stage in which hope looks to a future renewal of the Davidic dynasty. God will raise up a king who will establish a vast kingdom, secure and prosperous.

> For to us a child is born,
>   to us a son is given;
> and the government will be upon his shoulder. . . .
> Of the increase of his government and of peace
>   there will be no end,
> upon the throne of David, and over his kingdom,
>   to establish it, and to uphold it
> with justice and with righteousness
>   from this time forth and for evermore (Isa 9:6-7).

In this second stage the prophets present a hope that is more religious and more universal in scope. Salvation means the creation of a new Israel through the imparting of a new spirit that brings responsiveness to God's will (Jer 31:31). The prophetic vision sometimes expands beyond a purely nationalistic hope to a vision of universal peace in which all nations submit in obedience to God, who is revealed to them through the witness of Israel. God's intervention will be like a second creation, bringing about a second paradise and a new exodus:

> "I am the LORD, your Holy One,
>   the Creator of Israel, your King."
> Thus says the LORD,
>   who makes a way in the sea,
>   a path in the mighty waters.
> "Remember not the former things,
>   nor consider the things of old.
> Behold, I am doing a new thing" (Isa 43:15-16, 18-19).

But when the renewal of the Davidic dynasty does not come to pass, hope for future salvation moves into a third stage. At some point in the indefinite future the Lord will intervene and definitively establish the reign of God in the world. An ideal human ruler will be the instrument of the Lord in a glorious, final restoration of the nation. The Lord will endow with peace and prosperity all who acknowledge his rule and live in accordance with his will. Indeed, more than a restoration, the Lord will establish a new heaven and a new earth, with the whole of created reality in harmony and peace:

> On this mountain the LORD of hosts will make for all peoples a feast of fat things, a feast of wine. . . . He will swallow up death for ever, and the Lord GOD will wipe away tears from all faces, and the reproach of his people he will take away from all the earth (Isa 25:6-8).

In the first phase of eschatology, although the prophets often use cosmic imagery to speak of a dramatic renewal, the focus is on a future within history. But in time, when it seems that the reign of God will not come to pass in history, there is a second phase in the development of eschatology. Prophetic hope looks to a divine intervention to establish the kingdom of God in a transcendent realm beyond history. The second phase of eschatology is called "apocalyptic."

APOCALYPTIC ESCHATOLOGY

The name apocalyptic, from the Greek word for unveiling or revelation, denotes a specific literary form. In apocalyptic literature, writing about the end time takes the form of a special revelation in which a seer is granted a preview of the end time and its culmination in a transcendent world. Apocalyptic pictures the coming of God's reign as a dramatic intervention of cosmic proportions, in which the historic struggle between good and evil reaches its climax. The Lord definitively vanquishes the power of evil, puts an end to sin and death, and establishes an everlasting kingdom. Because apocalyptic uses fantastic imagery, it would not make sense if taken literally. But the powerful imagery does serve to arrest attention, so that apocalyptic prompts serious concern about the future, calls the people to account now for actions that will be subject to future judgment, and consoles with hope those who are presently undergoing trial for their faith.

Apocalyptic, however, is not distinctive simply because of its literary form. The theological content communicated through the literary form is also distinctive, a significant development beyond previous eschatology. While prophetic eschatology envisioned God's universal rule, it looked to Israel's future in the world. In apocalyptic eschatology the coming reign of God is no longer a kingdom in this world. Apocalyptic eschatology looks to future fulfillment in a transcendent realm established by the sovereign Lord whose power transcends life and death. Human effort, human institutions yield only failure and tragedy. God is the only hope. The sovereign Lord will intervene in history, call all human works into a judgment that is universal in scope, and bring about a world transformed, a new creation. Thus, apocalyptic proposes as the goal of hope not a restoration of the nation, but a future beyond history. What is at stake is not the destiny of individuals or the nation, but of the whole of creation.

Apocalyptic did not develop among the Jews until quite late in the biblical period, and with it arose the notion of the resurrection of the dead. Death was looked on as a natural termination of life, unless it was untimely, in which case it could be judged a punishment of sin. In a time of crisis, the Maccabean revolt against Greek persecution, there appears the apocalyptic book of Daniel, where one finds an unambiguous reference to life after death: "Many of those who sleep in the dust of the earth shall awake, some to everlasting life, and some to shame and everlasting contempt" (Dan 12:2). Belief in the resurrection enables those being persecuted to remain faithful even unto death. Later, the question arises about the fate of those already dead. If there is to be a judgment that establishes universal justice, everyone must rise either for reward or for punishment.

In sum, development of the notion of the reign of God through prophetic and apocalyptic eschatology sets the stage for the preaching of Jesus. To refer to the kingdom of God is to speak of the sovereignty of God. God creates and sustains the world, acts in history to save Israel, and will, in the end, establish his saving rule over all the world. The apocalyptic interpretation of the kingdom as a "new creation" in a transcendent realm was to have a profound influence in shaping Christian eschatology.

The New Testament

The hope of Israel for the one who will inaugurate the reign of God finds fulfillment in the person of Jesus. All of the Gospels identify Jesus as the Messiah (in Greek, "Christ"), the anointed one who succeeds in the line of King David. And at Jesus' crucifixion, the Gospels report, Pilate had this inscription posted on the cross: "This is the King of the Jews" (Luke 23:38).

The coming of the reign of God was the specific form in which Jesus preached God's saving action in history. In the Gospels Jesus uses the expression ninety times. Jesus shaped the notion of the kingdom in light of his experience of God and his own mission.

Jesus understood himself to have a special relationship with God. He also associated the breaking into history of God's reign with his own ministry: "Then turning to the disciples he said privately, 'Blessed are the eyes which see what you see! For I tell you that many prophets and kings desired to see what you see, and did not see it, and to hear what you hear, and did not hear it'" (Luke 10:23-24). At the end of Matthew Jesus declares his unique authority:

> ' All authority in heaven and on earth has been given to me. Go therefore and make disciples of all nations, baptizing them in the name of the Father and of the Son and of the Holy Spirit, teaching them to observe all that I have commanded you; and lo, I am with you always, to the close of the age (Matt 28:18-19).

THE MEANING OF THE KINGDOM

What does the reign of God mean? What shape will the fulfillment of human hope in the kingdom of God take? To answer these questions there is no one, tidy formula. The reign of God is too rich a notion for concise definition. Evidently Jesus presupposed a general notion of the reign of God to be familiar to the people he addressed. To appreciate the specific form Jesus gave to it one must consider all that Jesus said and did to announce the reign of God, and especially the death and resurrection that are the culmination of his life and ministry.

Jesus instructs his followers about the kingdom through his parables ("The kingdom of God is like . . ."). His stories reveal that God is compassionate love, uncalculating in generosity and forgiveness. God cares for the sinners, the poor, the sick, the disenfranchised. God's love is universal.

God gratuitously forgives the sinner. God is like a shepherd who leaves ninety-nine sheep to find the one that is lost (Luke 15:3-6); like a woman who searches diligently to find a lost coin (Luke 15:8-9); like a father running out to greet a wayward son (Luke 15:11-32). Jesus is explicit about the point of these stories: "There will be more joy in heaven over one sinner who repents than over ninety-nine . . . who need no repentance" (Luke 15:7).

One parable that forcefully tells the generosity of God is a story about a landowner (Matt 20:1-16). To day-laborers who had worked only one hour the landowner gives the same wage as to those who had worked the whole day. The other laborers object, but the owner asks them not to be envious because he is generous. By Jesus' account the justice of God means not quid pro quo, but open-handed generosity.

Perhaps no teaching more dramatically focuses on the indiscriminate nature of love in God's reign than the call for the forgiveness of enemies (Matt 5:44). Disciples are called to reflect the compassionate forgiveness of God (Matt 18:21-35). It is a way of living that Jesus himself poignantly exhibits on the cross when he turns to comfort the repentant thief crucified alongside him.

Jesus' conduct provides parables in action, which effectively present what he teaches. He dines, for example, with sinners and tax collectors. When others object he answers, "Those who are well have no need of a physician, but those who are sick; I came not to call the righteous, but sinners" (Mark 2:17).

In his embrace of the disenfranchised Jesus shows the way God means to reign, to be effective in the world. Jesus reaches out to all: as with sinners and tax collectors, so too with lepers (Luke 11:14), with Samaritans (Luke 17:11-19), with Gentiles (Matt 8:5-13). Jesus' ministry reveals the inclusive nature of God's reign.

God is close to us as unique individuals. This is clear from Jesus' teaching about providential care: "Why, even the hairs of your head are all numbered" (Luke 12:7). The parables about the lost sheep, the lost coin, and the lost son make the same point.

Just as instructive is Jesus' example, in his varied responses to individuals, like his humorous call to Zacchaeus to climb down from the sycamore tree and invite Jesus to dinner (Luke 19:5).

God's saving love embraces the whole of the person, soul and body, as an individual and in society. The reign of God is not a matter of a detached, purely interior or spiritual dimension of life. As Jesus forgives sin, so too he cures the sick, feeds the hungry, restores the lame, gives sight to the blind. In responding to the needs of others, Jesus does not treat them as isolated individuals. A person's dignity and membership in community are at stake. Jesus heals a woman bent double for eighteen years and thereby restores her dignity as a "daughter of Abraham" (Luke 13:10-17). Jesus cures a demoniac and sends him back to his people (Mark 5:1-20). These healings and exorcisms have removed the need for isolation from family and the larger community.

The teaching of Jesus intensifies the sense of social solidarity that informed the life of his people. The solidarity Jesus promotes has its source in God's love and manifests God's reign. Love of God means love of neighbor. Even the Law must bend: the Sabbath was made for man. Indeed, in Matthew's account Jesus focuses the whole of God's judgment on care of neighbor (Matt 25:31-46).

In the ministry of Jesus, then, the reign of God touches the whole person, both interiorly and physically, both as an individual and as an integral member of society. It is inclusive of all. Where such a story of love works its way, a new order of life, the reign of God, is working its way. Freed from self-centeredness and selfishness, our relationships are reconstituted, with respect to God and with respect to one another in human society:

> The proclamation of Jesus reveals that God is a saving God whose coming will effect personal and social transformation. A God whose reign will mean "good news," particularly for those who have experienced oppression (Luke 6:20-23). A God whose coming will, therefore, call for decisive response and whose appearance will create crisis and provoke judgment for those whose way of life is not in accord with the reality of that reign.[2]

The rule of God is the rule not of manipulative power, but of self-giving love that is uncalculating, all-inclusive, and, as Jesus' fidelity unto death demonstrates, without reserve.

JESUS' INAUGURATION OF THE KINGDOM

In announcing the advent of the kingdom the Gospels maintain a tension between present and future. The reign of God is a present reality because God acts decisively in the person of Jesus. The reign of God is a future reality because the kingdom that Jesus inaugurates will be fully established only at the end of time.

The beginning of Mark's Gospel illustrates God's sovereign action in Jesus with a dramatic sequence of extraordinary activity by Jesus. Everything happens with striking rapidity, all are amazed, and Jesus' unique authority gets special notice. In Luke, Jesus begins his ministry by quoting the prophecy of Isaiah:

> The Spirit of the Lord is upon me,
> because he has anointed me to preach good news to the poor.
> He has sent me to proclaim release to the captives
> and recovering of sight to the blind,
> to set at liberty those who are oppressed,
> to proclaim the acceptable year of the Lord (Luke 4:18-19).

He then declares: "Today this scripture has been fulfilled in your hearing" (Luke 4:21). Jesus explicitly associates the breaking in of the reign of God with his ministry: "But if it is by the finger of God that I cast out demons, then the kingdom of God has come upon you" (Luke 11:20). The new age has already begun in the present.

At the same time, the fullness of the kingdom lies in the future. Jesus teaches his disciples to pray for the coming of the kingdom (Luke 11:2). Many passages regarding judgment point to the arrival of the kingdom as a future event (e.g., Matt 13:24-30, 36-43).

Initially, the expectation is that the future kingdom will be established soon. There is a sense of urgency in Jesus' preaching. He regularly exhorts to watchfulness (Matt 25:1-13). The offer of salvation requires a decisive response: Jesus calls people to radical conversion and unqualified commitment (Matt 10:32-33). Failure to respond will bring condemnation (Matt 13:47-50).

On the one hand, the dynamism of God's reign has effect now, like yeast in dough (Matt 13:33) or seed in soil (Mark 4:3-9). It works its way quietly, but effectively. In answer to a question about the arrival of the kingdom Jesus declares, "The kingdom of God is in the midst of you" (Luke 17:21). On the other hand, Jesus instructed his disciples to pray for God's kingdom to come (Matt 6:10), although when that day will be "no one knows, not even the angels of heaven, nor the Son, but the Father only" (Matt 24:36).

THE KINGDOM TO COME

As we have seen, in the time before Jesus' mission the hope was for a definitive intervention by God. Some looked to a new heaven and earth in a transcendent realm. Others conceived the reign of God as having two dimensions: a heavenly realm, already established, from which God rules over history on earth; and an earthly kingdom, yet to come, in which an ideal king rules wisely over Israel and the nations.

It seems that during Jesus' mission the expectation was for a fulfillment on earth of the reign of God inaugurated by Jesus, though there was no precise definition of its form or the time of its fulfillment. It is likely that Jesus himself thought of God as reigning in heaven and the reign of God as making its presence felt through Jesus. Jesus probably looked for a future in which God's rule on earth would be complete. But for Jesus' disciples hope in the reign of God preached by Jesus seemed to die with Jesus on the cross (Luke 24:21). Then, after the resurrection, hope for the reign of God reawakened as hope for the Second Coming of Christ from heaven.

After Jesus' resurrection his disciples focused on the unique role of Jesus in God's plan of salvation. They proclaimed the risen Jesus to be Messiah and Lord. But the one raised as Lord and Christ is the one who preached the kingdom of God. Thus the disciples came to appropriate Jesus' teaching about the kingdom in light of the resurrection. The Second Coming might have meant, in the minds of some, that Jesus would rule the earth. But the hope for a transcendent destiny beyond history set the context for accepting and defining the meaning of Jesus' resurrection. Jesus' resurrection revealed the full meaning of the reign of God: eternal life in communion with God.

Early on, then, the Christian community transferred the peace and prosperity of Jewish expectation on earth to the reign of God in heaven. They summoned converts to join the community of faith, follow Christ, and share in the life of God's reign inaugurated by Jesus. They looked for the return of Christ to establish the reign of God in its heavenly fullness.

At first, the early Christian community expected that the Second Coming of Christ would be quite soon. After all, Jesus himself had preached that the reign of God was at hand. Added to that, dramatically dispelling the disciples' despond over Jesus' apparent defeat in death, was their experience of his resurrection. In due course, however, they came to realize the import of Jesus' saying about the end time: "But of that day and hour no one knows, . . . but the Father only" (Matt 24:36).

Thus, there is a tension in the New Testament when it treats the advent of God's reign. The tension arises because the reign of God arrives with Jesus but does not arrive in its fullness either in the resurrection of Jesus or soon after it.

When presenting the story of Jesus, each of the Gospels provides its own perspective and slant. Mark, Matthew, and Luke tell of the future coming of the Son of Man in judgment to inaugurate the fullness of the kingdom. Mark stresses the nearness of the kingdom, the final battle against evil, and preparation for the Second Coming. Matthew attends more to the resurrection and the presence to the Christian community of the risen Lord, who will fully exercise kingship at the end of the world. Luke, like Matthew, stresses the current presence of the risen Lord in the indefinite period before the coming of the Son of Man. He emphasizes the sending of the Holy Spirit, which is like a first form of the Second Coming. John, on the other hand, does not focus on the future, but on the present. Judgment takes place now, in one's decision about faith in Christ. Those who believe participate now in eternal life (an expression that is John's substitute for "reign of God").

Paul initially looked to the Second Coming as more or less immediate, but soon developed an already-but-not-yet perspective. The reign of God is already present and effective: "For the kingdom of God does not mean food and drink but righteousness and peace and joy in the Holy Spirit" (Rom 14:17). And for those who have the "first fruits of the Spirit" (Rom 8:23), there is a pledge of future glory (2 Cor 5:5), but the glory is not yet. The full flowering of what God began in Christ, the "firstborn among many brethren" (Rom 8:29), lies in the future when Christ "delivers the kingdom to God the Father" (1 Cor 15:24). In sum, the tension between a present inauguration and future completion of the reign of God that we know in the ministry of Jesus continues in the early Christian proclamation of Jesus' lordship.

What cannot be denied, and what continues to challenge successive generations of Christians, is the vivid sense the early Christian community had of the presence of the risen Lord to them through the Spirit and the intensity with which Christians should live in hope for the fullness of the kingdom. Again and again, we proclaim the death of the Lord in the Eucharist and pray for the coming of the kingdom, as we "wait in joyful hope for the coming of our Savior, Jesus Christ." The Eucharist we celebrate now not only proclaims the basis for our hope in the death and resurrection of Christ and gives us the food for our pilgrimage, it also anticipates the reconciling, unifying banquet originally signaled and promised when Jesus dined with sinners.

5

Talk of the End Time

Eschatology presents special challenges. First, the end time does not yet exist, so we ask on what basis we are able to speak about it. Second, although the end time lies beyond history, all the images and ideas used in speaking of it are drawn from everyday life in history. So we must establish a way to interpret the images and concepts that traditionally have been used to speak of the end time.

The Basis for Talk of the End Time

Divine revelation provides the basis for talk of the end time. The victory of the risen Christ gives us the irrevocable promise of future fulfillment in eternal life. Since Scripture provides the normative account of God's promise in Christ, Scripture is the basic resource for knowledge of the end time. We also have the teaching that the Church has elaborated on the basis of revelation.

But future fulfillment exists for us now only as a promise. We cannot know in specific detail when and how the promised reign of God will be fully established, or what concrete shape the kingdom of God will take. The future relationship between the world and God depends on the freedom of humankind and the freedom of God. Human freedom is making its way in a still uncompleted history, but what we accomplish now in freedom, and what our ultimate future with God will be, both depend fundamentally on the incalculable freedom of God.

Further, the movement beyond history into the eternity of God will involve a radical transformation of persons and the world. We lack any experience of what that transformation will produce. Scripture expresses ideas about the end time in language rich with concrete images and metaphors (judgment as a courtroom scene, heaven as a banquet, etc.). But we would err if we took such images literally. We would inevitably think of eternal life as a continuation of life as we know it in history, whereas the shape of life in the eternity of God will differ radically from our experience in history.

Consider a play. Knowledge of developing plot lines sketched by a dramatist does not imply knowledge of the specific sets, particular movements, actual dialogue, and concrete details of the denouement. Neither can talk of the end time describe the future as though scripted in detail and fully played out. Any attempt to talk of the end time in literal detail, as though we could know the future as we know the present, would be misguided. That attempt would misunderstand the kind of language used in Scripture to talk of the end time, as though it came from notes taken by a journalist who was transported beyond history to a briefing in heaven. Paul has the last word on the subject when he writes that the gifts God bestows are "what no eye has seen, nor ear heard,/ nor the heart of man conceived" (1 Cor 2:9).

The key to talk about the end time lies in not identifying the content with the form in which it is presented. We have to distinguish concrete images from the essential ideas that the images convey. Consider, for example, a stained glass window that represents the judgment of Christ at the end time. The window, unlike a photograph, cannot capture the specific detail of an actual scene. The picture presents a concrete image drawn from our present experience of a judicial exercise, but the seams of lead remind us of the inadequacy of the picture. While we necessarily conceive the end time and eternal life with the help of images, we have to fracture the images if we are to use them maturely, leaving both a picture and a reminder of its inadequacy. We must think critically about what the images mean to suggest if we are to understand them correctly.

The point is not to dismiss the cluster of images presented in Scripture and developed in Church teaching. Images suggest what eludes our conceptual grasp. Concrete images are powerfully evocative and formative, shaping a person's fundamental vision. Consider how frightful depictions of judgment, purgatory, or hell can distort the religious experience of people whom they terrify. Precisely because images shape our operative vision, we need to examine critically the language we use to talk of the end time.

The distinction between essential content and imaginative expression is not rigid. As creatures of the world, we can never get beyond concrete images in our thinking. The challenge, then, is to interpret scriptural texts and Church teaching in a way that respects the difference between images drawn from life in history and the reality of eternal life beyond history. The point is to articulate the meaning of traditional notions in language that, while faithful to their essential meaning, renders them intelligible and meaningful to people of contemporary culture.

A Method of Interpretation

We are creatures of time. We move into a future through a present that is based on a specific past. From our understanding of ourselves as presently moving into the future we can generate a prospective view of the future. Thus, statements about the end time articulate what we anticipate in the future based on our present experience of the promise of salvation in Christ. Reflection on experience in the world does not replace revelation with human speculation. The point, rather, is to interpret divine revelation aright and appropriate it. An example from everyday life will clarify the interplay of ordinary experience and divine revelation. A person is unhappy, restless, hurting in some way that is difficult to define. The person lives with some deep, unfulfilled need. Then the person falls in love. The experience of love strikes a person at heart and opens a whole new level of life and joy. Obviously, the gratuitous gift of someone's love comes as a surprise, something one could not program or predict. Yet, it responds to a basic human need. It obviously "fits" who the person can be. At the same time, the new-found love lights up and clarifies the capacity and need within the person. On the one hand, love clarifies the experience of need. On the other hand, the now clarified experience of need enables us to explain the meaning and importance of love.

So it is with God's revelation. Revelation fits our experience. Though it tells us something we do not figure out on our own, the revelation, when heard, rings true. This is not surprising since the revelation is for us and for our salvation. It would make no sense to us unless it somehow speaks to our experience, meets some elemental human need and desire. On the one hand, revelation clarifies our hope. On the other hand, examination of our experience clarifies how revelation responds to our hope for a fullness of life.

Similarly, our present experience allows us to anticipate, however inadequately, the what and the how of the end time. The yearning to move beyond what frustrates or hurts us to find full and definitive completion of what we can most fully be—that yearning helps us understand the substance of our hope. We also know from our experience the elemental dynamics of human living that move us toward fulfillment. Through analysis of fundamental human yearning and the dynamics of personal living, illumined by God's revelation in Christ, we can elaborate the general shape, the plot lines, of what we anticipate for our ultimate future.

Of course, reflection on what we anticipate in the present cannot add new information to God's promise of eternal life or provide concrete details about the shape of the ultimate future. Reflection on what we anticipate in the present provides a way to understand that promise.

The parameters for reflection are two: continuity and difference. There is a continuity between our life in the world now and the life in the world as perfected in the reign of God. Our experience now of God's gift of self in grace anticipates the fully established reign of God. As one author puts it, heaven "is not another world; it is the future of this world of God's creation, transformed by the creative power of God."[1] Ultimate fulfillment means that God's reign is fully and finally realized in a perfected world. Fulfillment of only part of our nature would mean either that our nature had been changed or that our fulfillment had been truncated. We must affirm an eternal future for the whole person as both spiritual and material, as both an individual and a member of one human race, as part of one cosmos.

But there will be a radical transformation that distinguishes the concrete shape of life beyond death from the shape of our experience in history. Death means the ending of life as we know it within history for participation in the eternity of God. We are misguided, then, if we think of eternal life as life in space and time as we experience them now. So, for example, we can affirm that heaven and hell do not literally designate places such as we inhabit now in history; rather, they are metaphors that express a definitive relationship with God in eternity. But in terms of positive description, we are left only with Paul's assertion that "no eye has seen, nor ear heard,/ nor the heart of man conceived,/ what God has prepared for those who love him" (1 Cor 2:9).

Those general guidelines can help us clarify traditional notions of the end time and correct misconceptions. We turn then to a consideration of the relationship between history and eternity.

6

Freedom, History, and Eternity

One day a happily married mother of five children remarked to me quite spontaneously, "You know, I really do not look forward to heaven." I must have looked alarmed because she began to laugh but then she explained what she meant. Whatever the demands of family life, she is having a wonderful time. Her husband is great and her children are a constant source of deep joy. As she imagines eternal life, it looks to be, well, boring. Why would she want to leave such an interesting, happy life for that?

To understand the continuity between history and eternal life we need to reflect further on human freedom: freedom in time (history) and the fulfillment of freedom beyond time (eternal life).

There are two ways to think about time. We can think of time as something external to us, a span marked off by clock and calendar. In that way of thinking, time is a context within which we live. We can also think of time as something interior, a quality of personal experience. In fact, interior time is the basis for external time. Only self-conscious persons who stand above the succession of events around them can mark time, can do the counting required for external time. Persons give meaning to time by making a history through their choices.

We are creatures of time. We move out of a past through a present into a future. Both the past and the future work their way in the present. The past, because it has shaped us and thereby influences our choices in the present; the future, because what we anticipate directs our choices in the present. Actually, however, only the present exists. The past and future are real for us only through the present, in which they become influential in memory and anticipation. Memory of the past and anticipation of the future make us explicitly aware of ourselves as creatures of time.

Moreover, because we are self-conscious, we do not merely survive between what has been and what might be. We are not caught in a flow of external time that carries us along like logs in a river. We are aware that we must make choices. We must take a stand toward the future, choosing this possibility or that. The need to choose makes us acutely conscious that we are creatures of time.

What is time about? What makes history? Choices make history. That is why plants and animals do not have a history in the proper sense of the term. They do not make choices. Their lives are automatic. But persons, by their choices, shape a story.

In a story there is a beginning, a middle, and an end. But the end is crucial. Without an end we could not designate a beginning. We cannot say, "It all began," unless there is an it, and there is no it unless successive moments culminate in a conclusion. We can say of a marriage, for example, that it all began because successive encounters culminated in a decisive commitment. Only in relation to an end can there be a beginning of *something*. And only in relation to the end can there be a middle. Without an end successive moments would be only a series of disconnected happenings. Any choice would be as good as another since no choice would count for anything. Because they lead to some conclusion the successive moments of a story are meaningful. That is one reason stories console us. They give a sense that there is some meaning and depth in our day-to-day lives. Each day contributes to the development of a meaningful plot.

Thinking about history as a story with an end helps us understand the relation of time to eternity. As long as our options remain open, there is still time. We have not yet brought our story to a conclusion, that is, we have not fully and finally defined ourselves. But fascinating as an open future can be, time puts a frightening question to us: Will we always be on the way, only in the process of becoming someone, always undefined, with no substantial identity? Or can we succeed in being someone? We want at heart to accomplish something, to define ourselves, to be someone. That is why we reach moments where we want to get on with it, close a deal, sign a contract, make vows. We hope at heart for life that is substantive, beyond the open-ended process of becoming in time. Such a life has, indeed, been promised to us through the resurrection of Jesus, which reveals to us that we are called to eternal union with God. That brings us to a consideration of human freedom.

Freedom in Time and Eternal Life

Freedom is not only about things outside of ourselves, but also about ourselves. In the process of making a choice, options attract me because of the values in each. I ponder over these values and then choose one option in preference to others. In choosing one option, I give priority to the values in that option. By my choice, therefore, I construct a set of priorities, a value system. The value system is not an abstract philosophy. It is quite concrete. It is myself, who I choose to be. If, for example, a person consistently chooses to act kindly, that person does not remain the neutral perpetrator of kind deeds. We do not say that person does kind things. We say the person is kind. Particular choices create and express some deeper choice about who we want to be. This deeper choice may be called our "fundamental option." In and through particular choices we opt for a basic style of being, we shape a concrete identity and define ourselves.

Freedom, then, is the capacity to define ourselves. If it were not so, what would the point of our choices be? We would never succeed in making something of ourselves, in being something. We do not make choices *in* the course of life; rather, our choices establish the course of life, our choices shape our story, make and define our being. Freedom is for something complete and definitive. The fruit of *becoming* through time is *being* in eternity.

The freedom to choose, then, defines the meaning of time and significant time as interior, personal time. In a broad sense, of course, time includes external, objective time, that is, the on-going, developing reality of the world that we can measure by clock and calendar. But the world has personal meaning through people. It is to personal time, the time of freedom and history-making, that we must look if we are to talk of the relationship between time and eternity.

Eternal life is life in a new mode of freedom. It is life whose past we have already given its final meaning and whose future holds no more open-ended options. Rather, it is freedom that has achieved a definitive identity. As time is a mode of existence in which there is a before and after in relation to choices in the present, so eternity is a mode of existence without such a before and after. As time is a mode of existence in which we are not yet in complete possession of ourselves because we are still in a process of becoming, so eternity is a mode of existence in which we enjoy completion and full self-possession.

Thus, there is continuity between time and eternity. But between time and eternity there is also discontinuity. Eternity is not freedom in process, but freedom fulfilled.

The moment in which we move out of time into eternity is death. Death ends our history in the world and the possibility of further choices that would shape our fundamental option. In death freedom takes its final form. Death is not the renunciation and abandonment of our history. Rather, our history comes to fulfill-ment in the movement through death into eternity.

The relationship between time and eternity becomes clearer when we consider our relationship with God in freedom.

Freedom, God, and Eternal Life

Ultimately our fundamental option is about God. Of course, we do not meet God face to face like someone on a street corner. But a response to God is implicit in our particular choices because our choices are always a response to something in God's world. In choosing to be in a certain way I implicitly either ratify or deny the creative will of God. Further, we do not relate to God only through the object of choice. God is not some impersonal context in which we choose. As we have seen, the underlying dynamic in the act of choosing is a relation to God that defines and summons us at heart. At work in our choices is a reach to God. Both in what we choose, therefore, and by the dynamics of choosing, we are always responding to God's offer of love. We act in faith and hope and love or else we choose self-centered and sinful denial of God. That is our fundamental option. We must, in the end, through our fundamental option, either be with God or alienated from God and God's creation. And this fundamental option is for eternity.

Eternal Life

Eternal life will be unqualified bliss in the inexhaustible vitality of communion with God and the whole of glorified creation. How can we imagine such wondrous vitality? Some authors dismiss talk of a quasi-temporal duration or a quasi-spatial situation for life after death. They argue that in the resurrection we participate in the eternity of God, citing what Paul has to say about spiritual bodies. Paul contrasts life in history, which is sinful and mortal, subject to corruption and death, with life beyond sin and death, life that is glorified. In that context he says what is sown is a physical body, what is raised is a "spiritual body" (1 Cor 15:44), free from the constraints of space and time.

Of course, in dismissing talk of a quasi-temporal duration or a quasi-spatial situation these authors do not reduce eternal life to a fixed state of being. In eternal life, Paul writes, "faith, hope, love abide" (1 Cor 13:13). Eternal life means the inexhaustible vitality of living into eternal communion with God and one another in a new creation. But for that very reason other authors insist on talking of duration. If life is on-going, must not eternal life entail some sort of duration? They also speak of a spatial dimension in the fulfillment of life in this world. Some reflections on time and space might be helpful at this point.

Time and Eternal Life

Significant time has to do with freedom that is open-ended, with shaping an identity by choosing among options. In that sense, there will be no time in eternal life. The time of choosing will have reached a wondrous fulfillment in the timelessness of a decisive commitment. Participation in eternal life would mean a self-possession that precludes any further change in personal identity. Thus, we should focus our conception of eternity on intensity of life rather than on temporal extension.

And yet, how can there be vitality without change of some sort? Is there no change inherent in the vitality of commitment in faith, hope, and love? Would we not be conscious of the succession of our interior acts and so in some sense experience duration and change?

We may find an answer to these questions if we reflect on certain experiences in which we seem to anticipate the experience of life outside of time. One of these we have already noted. In our self-consciousness we stand above the series of changes in life. We gather in the present a unity of past, present, and future through memory and anticipation. This gathering into a unity of the flow of time is an anticipatory experience of the way in which making history through choice in time finds its definitive culmination beyond time.

A second experience concerns the substance of life, not just its movement. There are acts in which persons gather together their very being with a decisiveness that is totally definitive. Think of an act of heroism, whether a single dramatic gesture (like falling on a hand grenade to save one's buddies), or a heroism played out through the drama of day-to-day living (like working two jobs to support special health care for a loved one), or an act of hope against all odds, or an act of fidelity despite deepest hurt. In such acts of freedom persons decide about themselves completely, unconditionally. In such acts they seem to define their being in a way that transcends the flow of time.

There are times, too, in our lives which seem to anticipate timeless, eternal vitality. Think of long hours spent in the company of good friends when we lose track of time. "Where did the time go?" Our sense of vitality at such times has more to do with the intensity of the experience than its extension in measurable time. The vitality was uninhibited, undistracted, focused, consuming.

Indeed, when looking back over our own story, we tend to focus only on significant time, not so much on externals as on time we made meaningful with other persons. We see this happen when good friends meet again after some years. Each one declares that the other has not changed at all, despite unmistakable weight gain, hair loss, and the advent of wrinkles. "You have not changed" means you are the same for me in personal stance and style.

The analysis just presented is only suggestive. There still remains a basic question. Eternity is a property of God. How can human persons ever have the kind of self-possession proper to divinity? Moreover, the analysis attends only to internal time, the vitality in personal consciousness. In eternity will there be external, objective time, that is, a succession in physical development that can be measured? There are those who argue that some sort of duration with a before and an after cannot be denied. But that only raises another question: In what sense would any "external" change be relevant? That question brings us to the issue of the spatial dimension of eternal life.

Space and Eternal Life

Persons are both spiritual and material, both individual and communal. They live in a shared context or space and are part of a material cosmos that finds its fulfillment in the fulfillment of humankind. If we take seriously the material dimension of human life, must not eternal life involve some sort of space? Speculation about space in the life of the world to come is as unavoidable as that about time.

As noted earlier, from Scripture we have only this, that Paul speaks of spiritual bodies. What does he mean by this paradoxical phrase? In the history of theology speculation on this point has been as endless as it is inevitable. In our own time, it is much less extensive, and certainly more muted.[1] The prevailing tendency of theologians in our time is simply to affirm the basic teachings about death and the resurrection of the body and to avoid further speculation. Perhaps we might rest with this simple affirmation: God, who calls us to intimate personal union in the eternity of God, is the time and the space of life beyond death.[2]

We turn now to the movement from history to eternal life through death and resurrection. In a later chapter we will return to the continuity between history and eternal life, focusing on hope in history.

7

Death

Death is the fundamental challenge to human hoping. Death brings to an end life in history. For some, the ending in death might be welcome because it gives relief from intense suffering. Others might welcome death because their life in this world has been long and full, and there seems to be no point in simply extending it. But commonly we resist death. It ends our time with others in this world, denies us the opportunity for further accomplishment, and terminates the only life we know. Even those who do not resist death must face the question: Does death mean the destruction of our history or its fulfillment? The Vatican Council II puts the issue straightforwardly:

> It is in the face of death that the riddle of human existence becomes most acute. Not only is man tormented by pain and by the advancing deterioration of his body, but even more so by a dread of perpetual extinction. He rightly follows the intuition of his heart when he abhors and repudiates the absolute ruin and total disappearance of his own person.[1]

It is true that the prospect of death can heighten our present sense of freedom and motivate us to live authentically. Death reminds us that the personal history we are currently creating is unique and irretrievable. But if life is simply terminated at death, what is the point of living authentically? Why should we take seriously a life that, in the end, will crumble into nothingness? The council admits that "the mystery of death utterly beggars the imagination."[2] The council affirms, however, that divine revelation dispels our anxiety in the face of death. Christ by his death has overcome the power of death. On the basis of that revelation Christians live in hope even in the face of death.

On death itself, the official teaching of the Church is quite limited. Two basic affirmations tell it all and can serve as an outline for a Christian understanding of death. First, death is the end of our earthly pilgrimage.[3] Second, death is due to sin.[4]

The End of Our Earthly Pilgrimage

To say that death is the end of our earthly pilgrimage can be misleading. One might imagine eternal life as a continuation of our present life. But *eternal* life is not a continuation of *temporal* life in history. As we have seen, in the process of shaping a history we establish a fundamental option. The result of our becoming through time is the definitive achievement of our relationship with God. This is why we have to die: the ending of earthly life in death is a movement into the eternity of God. Thus, death is not one more moment in a series of moments, distinctive only because it is the *last* moment on the calendar of life, nor is it simply a transition moment between temporal life and eternal life. Death, as we shall see, is the event *through* which, not *after* which, we achieve eternal life. Dying is not like getting off one train to board another. It is more like piloting an airplane down the runway and then taking off into an utterly different form of travel.

Death as a Personal Act

The traditional description of death as the separation of body and soul does not adequately indicate the personal character of death. In one respect, of course, death is impersonal. A human being has a physical structure. The disruption of that structure is something that happens *to* a human being. But there is more to a human being than a body. A person is not an object but a free subject who, within the limits set by human nature, chooses who she or he wants to be as a person. Since death affects the whole reality of a person, death is not simply something that comes upon a person from without, an event in which a person is merely passive. Dying is also something that happens from within; it is something a person does. Otherwise, the crucial event of death would not affect the human being as a person, as a free subject.

The personal aspect of death is this: in death one actively brings one's whole life to completion. Through time a person shapes a fundamental option. In death freedom takes its final form; the fundamental option becomes definitive. In death we bring our history of freedom to an end in a decisive act that recapitulates and brings to a culmination what we have been making of ourselves. That is why the event of death is not simply the final moment of temporal life, but also the fulfillment of temporal life in the beginning of eternity. We move into eternal life not *after* death, but *in and through* death.

Because death consummates our life in history, death is not a single, isolated event. Indeed, death is a life-long process, a dynamic at the heart of life. Throughout the history we shape, we live at heart in relation to the mystery of God. Insofar as we relate to God in faith and hope and love, our living is a dying. We die to our selfish selves, we die to selfish abuse of God's creatures, to selfish domination of life. This dying is an action: we give ourselves over in obedient surrender of everything to the will of God. Every moment in which we let go of ourselves in love of neighbor and God is a moment in the process of dying. Insofar as we commit ourselves in hope and trust to the will of God, we leave our selfishness behind. We put everything, including our very selves, at the service of love. To lose oneself to find oneself—that is the fundamental Christian option.

In the Christian view, therefore, the life-long process of dying is not simply becoming aware of our fragility and weakness, the acceptance of our inability to prolong our lives forever. For the Christian, dying is a life-long process of giving oneself in every *now* to the mystery of God, in hope of true life. The challenge is to find the fullest expression of our freedom in openness to the God of life, who is our future.

From the perspective of faith, then, death is not simply identical with clinical death. Human life is much more than biological life, and human death is much more than clinical death. In other words, we distinguish between death as the end of temporal life and death as the fundamental option to surrender oneself to the mystery of God. The moment of biological death need not be the moment that defines our relationship with God. Our fundamental option takes shape in the course of life. In the moment of bodily death the decision shaped throughout life achieves closure. Death consummates a life either of surrender to the mystery of God in hope or of self-centered determination to be in total control of our lives.

Death as the Effect of Sin

Logically it would seem that the death which terminates our life in history should not be something dark and fearful for us. Since we are called to eternal life, it should seem natural to find fulfillment in eternal life through an ending of our history in the world. But we experience death as something that ought not to be, something dark and frightening. Why the darkness in death, the fear of death?

The Church, following the New Testament, teaches that death, as we concretely experience it, is the consequence of sin. History has not been simply a story of gracious love. While God always extends love, we continually lead self-centered lives. And that human sinfulness leads to the darkness and fear in our experience of death.

As we have seen, because of the constitution of a human being as both nature (a given structure) and person (self-shaping freedom) death is an experience that is at once passive and active. In one sense, it is something that we do not choose. Against our will and in spite of every human effort, life leaves our body. But death is also something that we do; it is an active consummation of a whole life. This duality of passivity and activity makes death obscure. On the one hand, death is the act in which we bring ourselves to completion. On the other hand, death reduces a person to powerlessness. "Death appears both as act and fate, as end and

fulfillment, as willed and as suffered, as plenitude and emptiness."[5] Because of the dual aspects of activity and passivity in the
event of death, there is a frightening darkness in death. Will death
bring annihilation or human fulfillment?

Suppose that the human race had, from the beginning, been
fully responsive to God's gracious love. In that scenario, through
a gracious history we would develop a relationship with God in
complete integrity. All the dimensions of our being would be
drawn into the fundamental option of responsiveness to God in
faith and hope and love. Our call to eternal life would, of course,
involve our departure from history, but death would not be darkness for us. There would be no doubt about our eternal destiny, no
fear. We would willingly accept death as the way to achieve the
definitive fulfillment of what we have accomplished in our history.[6]

But it is not so. In our history we experience death as painful
darkness. Though the object of God's love, humankind asserts itself in self-centered, sinful rejection of God's will. Our freedom
works its way in a history infected by sin and our own sin com-
pounds the tragedy. The disordered pulls within us disturb the integrity we should have to develop our fundamental option, our
identity. Within us there is a tension between sinful self-assertion
and the summons of God's grace to die to our selfish selves and
find true life through commitment in faith and hope and love to
the mystery of God. The tension between sinful self-assertion and
faith in God is at its most heightened in the death that ends temporal life. Death challenges our self-determination in the most
radical way. And yet, when totally subject to a fate beyond our
control, we still have the choice of confronting death as emptiness
or as fulfillment. We can rebel against death or we can accept it
with hope in God. Death is an act which we perform: an act of
hope in the God of life or an act of despair.

Dying with Christ

In Jesus the mystery of God itself enters into the limitation,
vulnerability, and mortality of humankind. A man "who in every
respect has been tempted as we are, yet without sinning" (Heb
4:15), Jesus was subject to the effect of the sin that works its way

in the history he shares with us. He died in the darkness of death that is due to sin. The basis for Christian hope despite the darkness of death is the death of Jesus, for his death culminates in his resurrection.

If death for human beings is both passion and action, something suffered from outside but also an internal act that consummates a life, it must have been so for Jesus. As Scripture tells it, death came upon him from without: "Abba, Father, all things are possible to thee; remove this cup from me" (Mark 14:36). Jesus' death involved the deepest darkness and pain: "My God, my God, why hast thou forsaken me?" (Mark 15:34). But Jesus' death was a personal act. He accepted death out of fidelity to the will of God: "Not what I will, but what thou wilt" (Mark 14:36). He surrendered himself to the Father: "Father, into thy hands I commit my spirit!" (Luke 23:46). His death was the distillation and culmination of a life in obedience to the Father and fidelity to his mission.

Paul writes of Jesus that, for our sake, God "made him to be sin who knew no sin" (2 Cor 5:21). His death was not some act of arbitrary suffering imposed by God. It was the result of his fidelity to his mission in the face of the sin that thwarts the work of love. In apparent defeat of his mission, in rejection of his person, in the darkness and apparently godforsaken emptiness of death, he was steadfastly obedient in surrendering his life to God.

The cross of Christ stands as the sign of how completely God enters into human suffering. It is the sign of the self-emptying love of God. It is the sign that sustains our hope for the fullness of life through self-giving love in life and death. It is the sign that God means to assimilate us to the life and death of Jesus. Paul puts it tersely:

> But if we have died with Christ, we believe that we shall also live with him. The death he died he died to sin, once for all, but the life he lives he lives to God. So you also must consider yourselves dead to sin and alive to God in Christ Jesus (Rom 6:8, 10-11).

Because of sin the darkness that attends bodily death will not disappear. The death that ends our history can be a refusal of trust in God, a rebellion against our destiny, or an obedient surrender to the mystery of God, a personal appropriation of the death of Jesus. But if we conform our lives to that of Jesus, dying to self in love for others, we are already living by the grace of God, sharing in God's eternal life. As John puts it, "We know that we have passed out of death into life, because we love the brethren" (1 John 3:14). In that case, the death that ends our temporal existence will bring to its culmination a life of dying to self in faith and hope and love, making full and final our share in eternal life.

8

Resurrection

Hope in the kingdom of God has its basis in the resurrection of Christ, which inaugurates the reality of the kingdom in its fullness. So we consider now the teaching about resurrection: what we mean by resurrection, how we know of the resurrection through faith, and what the resurrection has to tell us about our hoping.

Resurrection: A Definition

The resurrection is the event in which God accepts Jesus fully into the dimension of God's eternal life and life-giving power. In the resurrection God definitively accepts the whole person of Jesus despite his apparent defeat and destruction in death: Jesus' understanding of himself and the Father, his teaching, his ministry, his whole life of filial obedience and service to God's people—all that God accepts, vindicates, and brings to fulfillment. Jesus becomes Lord, sharing the fullness of the Spirit and the Father's glory.

Jesus had an intimate personal relationship with the Father. His ministry revealed the prodigal love of the Father, who gives life and offers forgiveness to all. Jesus understood himself as inaugurating the reign of God. Through his healing of body and spirit, as well as through his preaching, he anticipated in his ministry and

identified with his person the long hoped-for future reign of God.
As a result of his claims and ministry he had to accept death. In
his death he bore the sin that led to his death and demonstrated
the will to reconciliation that lay at the heart of his message and
ministry. Despite the apparent failure of his ministry he died in
hope: "Father, into thy hands I commit my spirit!" (Luke 23:46).
His death was the definitive expression of surrender to the will of
the Father in fidelity to his mission, and hence was the consum-
matory expression of his filial relationship to the Father. In the
resurrection God established Jesus in the fullness to which his life
and death were oriented.

Jesus' Resurrection: A Culmination

It is important to situate the resurrection of Jesus as the culmination of Jesus' life and death. Why was *this* man raised from the
dead? Unless there were continuity of Jesus' resurrection with his
ministry and death, the resurrection would have no meaningful
context. It would appear as a bizarre happening, unintelligible to
Jesus' disciples. The designation of Jesus as Messiah and Lord
would be altogether arbitrary. But the resurrection is not some
magical episode added on to the life and death of Jesus. It is not
a reward selected by God to acknowledge Jesus' fidelity unto
death. It is not a miracle that proves the truth of Jesus' message.
Who Jesus was, and what he did—*that* is what God accepted in
the resurrection. When we understand that, we will grasp the
meaning of the resurrection.

Who Jesus was, what he said and did, what he became in the
course of his life—all of that culminates in his dying. In his death
Jesus brings to final and full concentration his life of filial obedience. As he decisively unites himself with God in self-surrendering
dedication, so his dying culminates in his resurrection. This point
is vividly expressed in a letter of Paul:

> He humbled himself and became obedient unto death, even
> death on a cross. Therefore God has highly exalted him and be-
> stowed on him the name which is above every name, that at the
> name of Jesus every knee should bow . . . and every tongue

confess that Jesus Christ is Lord, to the glory of God the Father
(Phil 2:8-11).

The Father's acceptance fulfills a relationship between Jesus
and the Father that formed the very life of Jesus. What appeared
to be Jesus' complete personal failure and the collapse of the mission tied to him is now revealed as telling the truth about God's
faithful love. But that revelation makes sense precisely because it
represents the culmination of Jesus' life, a life in hope of the kingdom, a life that embodied the compassionate, forgiving, healing,
reconciling love of God, a life in union with God. Such a life finds
its congruent fulfillment and its validation in union with the God
of self-giving love. The life of Jesus, therefore, makes intelligible
its culmination in resurrection, even as the resurrection vindicates
and fulfills that life.

Faith in the Resurrection

As an event, the resurrection is unique in kind. It brings a person to a new, qualitatively different mode of life. The whole reality of a person attains the fullness of life in immediate union with
God. On the one hand, the event is historical, since it happens at
a point of human history in the world. On the other hand, the
event is beyond history, since it is not a resuscitation and return
to life in history, but a movement beyond history. We cannot com-
pare it with other historical events. Because it is a unique kind of
event, the resurrection cannot be known or be empirically verified
in the manner of ordinary historical events.

Some find it troublesome that there can be no empirical verifi-
cation of resurrection. But if there is such an event, then we have
to respect the *kind* of event that it is. We can only know something
with the kind of knowing appropriate to the kind of thing it is. For
example, since God is not simply another person in the world, one
cannot know the reality of God the way one knows finite beings
in the world. Why? Because God is unknowable? No, but because
God is not the kind of reality that can be known in that way. Or,
to take an example closer to home, consider how we know other
persons. There are a lot of obvious things we can know about

them: height, weight, etc. But who they are at heart we can only know through faith, hope, and love. We can know them as persons, but only with the kind of knowing appropriate to realities that are incalculably free. The same holds true of the resurrection event. The transformation of a person taken out of history into the eternity of God cannot be empirically verified as though it were an ordinary historical event in the world.

Knowing the resurrection is necessarily a matter of faith, understanding faith here not as a deficient substitute for empirical knowing, but as a unique way of knowing a unique kind of reality. Consider all that is implicitly involved: faith in the reality of God, faith that God can and does act in history, faith in the possibility of immediate union with God. Such faith would have been essential for the disciples to acknowledge the risen Jesus. Without it, they would not have been open to knowing the risen Jesus any more than a person whose eyelids are closed can see a tree, or than a defensive person can see a would-be friend except as a threat. We often miss the signals sent by another because we are not open to the other's outreach.

Nonetheless, if the resurrection is to make sense to us it must somehow fit our experience. And so it does. The human person wants at heart to experience the fullness of life, the fullness of meaning and beauty and love. Further, we hope that our lives will be meaningful in some definitive way, beyond the flow of open-ended, indefinite time. There are many questions that we *have,* and there is the question which we *are.* The question that we are keeps us constitutionally restless until we get caught up into the fullness of meaning, beauty, and love. Hence, our openness in hope for the future is not openness to just this or that event. It is openness to the event of resurrection. The notion of resurrection speaks to the deepest desire and hope at the heart of us. It makes sense.

There is a circularity in our faith in resurrection. On the one hand, there is in us an elemental hope that opens us to news of resurrection. On the other hand, the news of resurrection clarifies the hope it satisfies. We have discussed this circularity before when reflecting on the dynamics of revelation. If we are disposed to reverence the human person as having a depth that is infinite in

capacity and reach, the notion of a resurrection event will not
seem bizarre, a primitive myth. In turn, news of the resurrection
summons us to appreciate the reach at the heart of us as a hope
for eternal life, and so clarifies the hope that alerts us to accept the
news.

There is another element in the dynamic of our faith in the resurrection. The original disciples faced the challenge of believing
in the risen Jesus who appeared to them. But we were not there,
so our challenge is a different one. We must have faith in the disciples' proclamation. If we are people of hope, we are disposed to
accept the news in faith. That is especially the case if we consider
the congruence of Jesus' resurrection with his life and ministry
and death. But the fact remains that the resurrection, of its nature,
can only be affirmed by faith: "Blessed are those who have not
seen and yet believe" (John 20:29). That faith depends on the hoping by which we reach out to find the fulfillment of our hoping.

At times the question is asked: Could Jesus' disciples be re-
porting as an objective event what is, in fact, a purely subjective
experience, a fantasy? Several points should be noted about the
witness of the disciples. First, the disciples' claim is unique. They
know it to be extraordinary. They do not accommodate their report to ordinary expectations. They report not *a* resurrection, but
the resurrection of *this* man, a man condemned, cast out, crucified. Second, the Gospels report the disciples' despond after
Jesus' death and their own doubt and confusion after the resurrection. Third, what they report has to do not with their subjective
response, but with what God has done in Jesus: Jesus is alive, in
a new way. Fourth, their proclamation does not simply have to do
with a cause that they need a risen Jesus to validate. In proclaiming the resurrection the disciples identify the cause with the risen
Jesus himself, proclaiming his reign. Jesus' resurrection defines
the meaning of the cause and inaugurates his rule as Lord. Fifth,
it should be noted that what the disciples affirm in the resurrection is not simply an event, however unusual. It is *the* event. In the
context of the eschatology of the time, which looked to a new
creation at the coming of God's reign, and in their own interpretation of the event, what they proclaimed in the resurrection had
to do with the collective destiny of all God's people. For that af-

firmation there must have been a powerful experience at base, both in the ministry of Jesus and in their Easter experience. Finally, it should be noted that Paul is careful to record the history of faith in the resurrection, noting the original appearances of Jesus to witnesses, which he distinguishes carefully from his own unique conversion. And Paul himself enjoyed a faith that met opposition, as is clear from his rejection by the Athenians who could not accept the notion of bodily resurrection.[1]

In dealing with the apostolic witness itself we must return again to the dynamic of faith in resurrection. Such faith is a matter of participation. Let me illustrate with the dynamic of love between persons. Love is a self-validating experience. Those in love do not need to verify it empirically. For those outside the relationship it cannot be verified. Love is not an empirical *kind* of reality, but is rooted in the mystery of freedom that cannot be exhaustively rationalized. Another example is provided by the experience of faith. To have faith in others does not entail a lack of objectivity. Faith is the *kind* of knowing that gives access to the *kind* of object grasped, in this case, other persons in their freedom. Through faith we gain access to a relationship that can only be appreciated within the relationship, within the sharing of life. So it was for the disciples of Jesus: through their faith in Jesus, alive and present, they entered into a new, life-giving relationship, and thus they experienced the power of his resurrection.

Resurrection: Body and Soul

From early on, Christian thinking about life after death has been deeply influenced by Greek philosophy. The ancient Greek philosophers disdained matter. They did more than distinguish body and soul; they divorced them. The Greeks held the true reality of a person to be the soul. Of course, the soul is bound up with a body during its time on earth, but the person (soul) will achieve its ultimate perfection when the soul is released from its entanglement in the material world. Thus, Greeks thought of life beyond death in terms of the immortality of the soul. That thinking has affected the Christian imagination deeply. No doubt, Christians were happy to appropriate Greek teaching about the immortality of the soul because it supported their hope for life beyond death, but that teaching brought with it the danger of a distortion of Christian hope.

The notion of resurrection differs significantly from the notion of immortality of the soul. The basic difference lies in an understanding of the person that comes from the biblical tradition. The biblical notion of the person does not involve a distinction of body and soul as two disparate parts, but as two dimensions of a single reality. When Scripture uses the word for one of the two dimensions, it nonetheless refers to the whole person. When, for example, Paul distinguishes flesh and spirit, he is not distinguishing body and soul within a person. Rather, he contrasts a person who is mortal, weak, and sinful with a person graced by God. Flesh refers to the whole human person, a unity that, taken by itself, is weak, mortal, sinful. Spirit is the life of grace bestowed by God on the whole person (flesh). Resurrection, therefore, means God's granting of life beyond death to the whole person, in both its spiritual and bodily dimensions.

The context of belief and anticipation in which the first Christians accepted the resurrection of Jesus is of vital importance. At the time of Jesus, belief in the resurrection did not mean belief in the immortality of the soul, but belief in the fidelity of God's love. Thus, the risen Jesus lives in the presence of God in his whole human reality.

To be sure, resurrection could not mean materiality as we now experience it, any more than eternity could mean an indefinite extension of life in history. But we find the basis of our hope for eternal life in the resurrection of Jesus, not in the philosophical speculation of the Greeks. Accordingly, the Creed affirms resurrection of the body, not immortality of the soul.

Further, the tradition of eschatology out of which Christian understanding of the resurrection arose was a tradition about the salvation of the individual as an integral member of humankind in a shared world. The prophets consistently decried infidelity to the covenant and injustice in society as the cause of Israel's degradation. When the Israelites looked to the Lord to intervene in history and establish the reign of God, they looked for the salvation of a whole people and of the world the people shared. They looked for a life of justice and harmony in a world with prosperity for all. They thought of themselves as a nation, a people. In time they came to see other nations as also called to share together with them a life in a new creation, a new heaven and earth.

This tradition stands in stark contrast with that of the Greeks. The Greek notion of the immortality of the soul implies disdain for matter and the body. But it is through materiality that the life of a person takes place in a shared world. To disdain the body is to disconnect persons from others and the world. The notion of the perfected person as essentially a disembodied soul inevitably carries with it a notion of the person that is essentially individualistic. In contrast, the hope for resurrection looked to the transformation of persons as members of a community in a transformed world, not to a collection of individual souls. Thus, Jesus' resurrection is not something that has as its focus only Jesus. Rather, it has universal significance. The resurrection signals the saving will of God for the whole of creation.

Great theologians of the Church made use of Greek philosophical concepts to develop an understanding of the faith. They make a distinction between body and soul and assert the immortality of the soul. But they do not understand body and soul as two independent parts assembled to make a composite. Rather, body and soul are essentially interrelated as matter and form. The soul is the form that gives specific character to matter, making it soul-informed matter, so that it is an ensouled body, somebody. The body is matter that, by receiving a specific kind of life and character, makes the soul an embodied soul, somebody.

In more recent times, theologians talk of the unity of spirit (soul) and matter (body) in terms of self-presentation or self-expression. To be human, to be a self in the world, to be with others in a shared history, I have to present myself in and through my body. It is only in and through my body that I succeed in being fully myself, because only in and through my body do I come to actual expression and full presence in the world. That is why we cannot speak simply of self *and* body. They are dimensions of a complex but unitary reality, a unity-in-complexity.

Think of all the expressions or self-embodiments by which we succeed in making not something else, but ourselves. We make gestures, we make conversation, we make covenants, we create societies and cultures. These self-expressions are not added to me. They are how I am a self, who I am. Through all these self-expressions we embody ourselves and become fully real as persons in a shared world. We are effectively present through expressive embodiment. Our bodies are the vehicle of worldliness and community. All the self-expressions by which we become fully real flow out of the basic human structure, a soul-body.

The Importance of Bodily Resurrection

In the notion of the resurrection as the summons to everlasting life of the whole person, not a disembodied soul, a great deal is at stake. The issue is not fidelity to traditional teaching, but what is at stake in the traditional teaching: our understanding of ourselves as persons, of our relationships with one another, of our world, of what we accomplish in history. If we imagine life beyond death as immortality of the soul, then our ultimate hope is not salvation of the world, of the history, of the community we have shaped, but salvation *out of* the world, beyond a history, with others left apart. The dualism that focuses on the immortality of the soul begets a disdain for the world, indifference to accomplishment in history, and a radical individualism that fractures the fundamental connection by which we were made to be ourselves precisely with one another in a shared history. But the resurrection of Jesus inaugurates the transformation of the whole of creation. Hence, resurrection hope means hope for society and the world. And, more than signaling a future destiny, it shapes life now. We are our authentically Christian selves only in a shared history. That is where we can act out our hope in the kingdom, like Jesus, even in the face of frustration and death.

9

Judgment

Hoping is a necessity for entrance into the reign of God. We cannot achieve this on our own or demand it from God. But for Christians to speak of the necessity of hope is needlessly abstract. God has already chosen to be "in Christ reconciling the world to himself" (2 Cor 5:19). To get a better sense of what that means let us consider our relationship with good friends. When we first meet them, our knowledge of them may be minimal and our faith in them only tentative. As friendship develops, our faith in them grows deeper and our hope gradually becomes trust. In the same way, God is not simply an abstract idea to us, but a concrete, personal reality, of whom the evangelist could write: "For God so loved the world that he gave his only Son, that whoever believes in him should not perish but have eternal life. For God sent the Son into the world, not to condemn the world, but that the world might be saved through him" (John 3:16-17). As our faith in this revealed God deepens and more fully informs our hoping, hope in God becomes trust in God.

But we, for our part, are free and freedom is a matter of *self*-definition. Through our personal history we make a fundamental option, shape our identity, and determine our ultimate destiny. But how can we definitively evaluate our fundamental option? Our history is not yet finished. Future choices might confirm the basic identity we have been shaping or they might initiate a turn-around. Prior to the end of our history, our identity remains provisional.

Moreover, we cannot accurately evaluate our own freedom. To do so we would again employ the very freedom we mean to evaluate. For we do not reflect with detached, impersonal minds. All of our thinking is done in accordance with the way we choose to be and choose to think. The final meaning of our choices always remains somewhat opaque to us.

And so, the culmination of our lives in death and resurrection requires a final judgment by God. This judgment decisively clarifies who we are before God and defines our eternal destiny.

Judgment: Particular and General

There are two dimensions to the final judgment, corresponding to two basic dimensions of the human person. A human person is both a unique individual and an integral member of the human community. Hence, we distinguish particular judgment and general judgment.

The notion of particular judgment speaks to the uniqueness of each person. Our individual stories are not parts of a drama in which all the roles are similar and the actors interchangeable. Each of us is called by name. Each of us has a meaning shaped through our original freedom. Each of us has an eternal destiny as a unique individual. It is fitting, then, that there be a final judgment that focuses on each of us as individuals.

The particular judgment, however, will be part of a general judgment that addresses humankind as a whole. The notion of general judgment speaks to the essentially social nature of persons. We are unique individuals only in community. The point is obvious if we think of our immediate families, which shape us as individuals and which we help to shape. It would take pages to list all the other communities of which we are members (nation, parish, business, school, etc.) and to articulate the connections between these communities. Most fundamentally, though, we are members of God's people, Christ's body. When we celebrate the Eucharist, we pray that God see us not as individuals, but as members of a whole people: "Look not on our sins but on the faith of your Church." The destiny of a human person is not a private one, but finds its full meaning in the destiny of humankind as a whole, the kingdom of God.

And so, the judgment and consummation of the individual contributes to the judgment and consummation of human history as a whole. Correlatively, the consummation of history as a whole embraces the consummation of the individual.

Imagining Judgment

Traditionally the images used to describe the judgment have been those of a courtroom. God sits on a throne before which we stand in fear and trembling. An account of our deeds is read. A judgment is handed down. We might be welcomed into the eternal joy of heaven or we might be consigned to an eternity in hell. The third possibility is that we might be sentenced to spend a period in purgatory, as punishment for our sins and as part of a purification process.

This dramatic picture captures the imagination and calls forth from us a serious response. We *should* get busy about giving some direction to our lives and making some contribution to the larger community. After all, we are going to be judged on how we have used these two talents entrusted to us.

The courtroom image of divine judgment, however, can be as dangerous as it is useful. True, at the heart of the awesome responsibility for our eternal destiny is a call of love, God's promise of the kingdom. Nevertheless, we know our self-centeredness and weakness. The awesome responsibility can become a crushing burden. That is why the courtroom image of divine judgment is so potentially misleading. We are in constant danger of understanding God, not by the word of God, but by our own word, by projections based on our way of thinking and acting. We can think of judgment as though it were a proceeding in a secular legal system instead of the decisive culmination of God's relationship with us.

To interpret the image of judgment correctly we must set it in its proper context in the preaching of Jesus. Jesus' ministry focuses on the kingdom of God. But there are moments when the depth of God's love and concern for us, and the seriousness with which God summons us, find dramatic presentation in talk of divine judgment. Even so, it is crucial to note that the context of talk about judgment is the constant, insistent preaching of what is at the heart of the gospel: compassion, mercy, forgiveness, reconciliation, and the coming of God's reign.

To be sure, there is a kind of judgment implicit even in compassionate love. The love of another for us exposes our own lovelessness. We become aware of our own self-centeredness by contrast. God's word of love is the same sort of two-edged sword: precisely as the offer of love, it elicits a sense of sin and unworthiness. That is why it is so fitting that we begin every celebration of the Eucharist with a Penitential Rite.

"Repent, and believe in the gospel" (Mark 1:15). Belief in the Good News requires repentance, an honest recognition of our inadequacy and need. We must admit that we are the sick to whom Jesus ministers, not the healthy "who have no need of a physician" (Matt 9:12). We might find this a daunting task, but the good news itself gives us the courage to carry it through. Love drives out fear. Because we have in the Good News the security and support of forgiving love, we can confront our failures. We are given the freedom to make an honest assessment of our lives. Set in the context of the Good News, talk of judgment should stimulate not slavish fear (which is self-protective and leads us to deny or minimize our faults), but reverential fear (which out of love for God wants to acknowledge any offense and seek reconciliation).

Judgment as Self-Judgment

In the traditional picture of the final judgment it is only then that we learn what God has decided in our case. But a Christian who believes in God's love would look at it very differently. After all, we are the ones who made all the choices that have fashioned our identity. In that perspective God's judgment simply confirms an identity we have already worked out for ourselves.

To understand how judgment is self-judgment, imagine what it would be like to meet Mother Teresa. We know that what touches us at heart is not talk, but example. Jesus' words at the Last

Supper about feet-washing service and about giving his body and blood for us were true, effective words because what he said he *did:* "I have given you an example" (John 13:15). In the presence of Mother Teresa we might feel ourselves judged, not because she was being judgmental, but because we feel the difference between her virtue and our own poverty of spirit. The fact that an encounter with another challenges us may be our doing, not theirs.

Consider another example. There are some gatherings at which I feel uncomfortable: "This is not my crowd." It is not necessarily the fault of the group. In fact, it might be an excellent crowd. But it is not mine. The differences between them and me make me feel ill at ease. There is no need to ask me to leave. I slip away of my own accord. I may have missed what turned out to be a great party, but that was not a penalty imposed on me from outside. It resulted from the kind of person I have become through my own choices.

What about those times when good friends criticize us? Should we think of that as a judgment from outside? No, good friends call us to account out of love and concern, not because they are judgmental. Self-righteousness is not an attribute of quality people, and certainly not of good friends. The focus in their chiding is on us and our future, and the point of it is to call us to a more authentic life. Indeed, the love we feel in their doing this opens us to hear their counsel and motivates us to change.

If Jesus' constant teaching and consistent way of acting is the decisive revelation of God, we know the goodness of God has nothing to do with self-righteousness (*that* is what Jesus insistently condemns). It has to do with compassionate love that means to forgive and bring reconciliation. Indeed, those most in need are the favored objects of Jesus' attention. Our need and hurt and weakness and sinfulness are precisely what God means to address. A Christian can only speak of judgment in the context of God's reconciling love. God's judgment has nothing to do with a desire to find fault, much less a desire to devise vindictive punishment. If we, at our best, are not vindictive, how could we imagine God being so? As with friends, a calling to account in the course of a relationship challenges us at heart and center. But the challenge is meant to be liberating, not humiliating.

Divine Judgment

So far we have discussed judgment from the perspective of our action. On that analysis, judgment may be described as self-judgment because it will clarify what *we* have made of ourselves in relation to God. But a deeper analysis shows how judgment is God's doing. First of all, we do not determine the timing either of our own death or of the end of history. In addition, as noted earlier in this chapter, we are not capable of making an accurate evaluation of our own freedom. Finally, it is for God to determine how God will deal with what we have made of ourselves.

What is the status of our fundamental option and our self-judgment in death? Does God simply confirm our judgment of ourselves? No, we do not define our eternal destiny on our own. Our self-definition is about a relationship with God. What we do always involves the creative, sustaining, and empowering love of God, in whom "we live, and move and have our being" (Acts 17:28). God works in and through us in ways we cannot calculate. Moreover, our doings do not determine the response of God. In death, too, we are subject to the freedom of God. God's judgment, then, is not simply an accounting and pronouncement of a condition already established. Christ's resurrection gives witness that at death the God of the living works a transformation and fulfillment of creation. The kingdom of God is fundamentally and finally God's doing and so, therefore, is the judgment that is an integral moment in God's final establishment of the kingdom.

What do we know of God's judgment? As a matter of historical fact and everlasting truth, God has decisively defined and clarified the destiny of human history. In the death and resurrection of Christ God's basic judgment on history has been revealed. Christ overcame sin and death: Christ "was put to death for our trespasses and raised for our justification" (Rom 4:25). Christ revealed that God's judgment is a life-giving judgment. Christians cannot be true to their faith and still think of history as somehow neutral in its basic meaning. Through the death and resurrection of Jesus, God has inaugurated the kingdom. Christians have good grounds for hoping and trusting that their judgment in death will share in God's transforming power over sin and death as revealed in Christ.

The End of History

The prophets of the Old Testament proclaimed a Day of the Lord, when God would intervene in history to vanquish the powers of evil and definitively establish the reign of God. The New Testament identifies that moment with the future coming of Christ, the Son of Man who will come in judgment. For this Second Coming of Christ the evangelists use the Greek term for arrival, *parousia.*

The expression Second Coming has merit. Only with the consummation of history as a whole will the kingdom inaugurated by Christ be fully established. We are essentially social beings, called to be members of one body of which Christ is the head (Eph 4:15-16), living stones of a spiritual house of which Christ is the cornerstone (1 Pet 2:4-7), branches of the one vine that is Christ (John 15:5). The fulfillment of an individual cannot be complete apart from the fulfillment of the whole of redeemed humanity.

Christian solidarity traditionally finds expression in the term "communion of saints." We make our way through a shared history in this world by hoping with one another, hoping in one another. That includes those who have died. They do not lose their connection with us. In Christ they have become "a new creation" (2 Cor 5:17). We live in and through a communion of saints, a communion rooted in our fellowship with Christ, a communion made up of both those living by the Spirit of Christ in our world and those already called into the company of the risen Christ. If we believe in the communion of saints, we believe that, as we do not live alone, so we do not die alone, are not raised alone, are not judged alone, and do not find fulfillment alone.

Talk of the Second Coming of Christ can be misleading in one respect. It might suggest a separation of the first coming of Christ (incarnation) from the second (judgment). Such a separation would obscure the fact that God has already inaugurated the kingdom and that the risen Christ is continuously present throughout history. Where the grace of God is effective in the world, the reign of God is already present, in movement toward future completion. The Second Coming does not mean the return of a Lord who has been absent. Rather, it will complete the work that Christ continues throughout history in the power of the Spirit. Indeed, we can think of the parousia as the world's coming to Christ. At the parousia the saving power of Christ at work in our history will achieve its final and full victory. The parousia will be "the appearing of the glory of our great God and Savior, Jesus Christ" (Titus 2:13).

Paul pictures the whole universe as eagerly awaiting this day, when it too "will be set free from its bondage to decay" (Rom 8:21). Creation, he says, groans like a woman in labor and we ourselves likewise groan inwardly as we wait for our common redemption: "For in this hope we were saved" (Rom 8:24).

We do not know when God will bring history to an end. In the Gospel of Mark Jesus says, "But of that day or that hour no one knows, not even the angels in heaven, nor the Son, but only the Father" (13:32). Some New Testament passages speak of signs that will precede the parousia. But scholars commonly understand those signs as present in all periods of human history.

How the consummation of history will take place we cannot conceive. The ending of history and the configuring of the new creation is a matter of the creative action of God. We live *within* a relationship to God, *within* the creative action of God. We cannot stand above our relationship with God and make divine creativity an object of study.[1] The consummation of history, as well as its origin, lies in the transcendent mystery of God. Zachary Hayes puts it tersely: "In the beginning, is God. In the end, is God and the fruit of history."[2]

10

Purification

People of faith live with a sense of their own sinfulness. Anxiety about their unworthiness before God can even temper their hope for eternal life. What happens to those who die, united with God in faith, hope, and love, but burdened with a sinfulness that renders them unfit for full communion with God? The Church teaches that such persons pass through *purgatory,* which is commonly pictured as a place of suffering where they are purified before entering into union with God. This doctrine reflects the constant practice of the Church, revelatory of its deepest faith, of praying in the liturgy for those "who have gone before us marked with the sign of faith."

Once again, as with all talk about the end time, we must distinguish concrete images from the essential meaning that the images should convey. The Council of Trent, which articulated Church doctrine about purgatory, affirmed authoritatively only two points: there is a process of purification, and the prayer of the faithful on behalf of the dead is a help to them. Trent does not teach anything about a place, a period of time, or the nature of the punishment. The essential point in the teaching on purgatory is the purification that is effected.

Given the love and mercy of God revealed in Christ, many Christians have difficulty with the notion of hell, but this is not the case with the teaching on purgatory. We already have some familiarity with the process of purification. We know what it is like to have an ideal and fail to attain it. We know too that our failures create new barriers we will have to overcome.

It may be helpful to approach this matter by speaking first about the goal of integrity, then about falling short of that goal, and finally about the resultant need of purification.

Integrity

Integrity means drawing the many dimensions of our personal being into line with one another. We say of persons of integrity that they have their act together. They bring their desires and actions into line with their chosen course. Whatever the complication and change in their lives, there exists a coherence and consistency in them. To become a person of integrity is not to become simplistic, narrow minded, or strait-laced, but to give oneself identity and substance.

Persons of integrity prompt us to pass judgment on ourselves. We sense the difference between their clarity and our confusion, between the convergence of their aspirations and the dispersion in our desires, between their constancy and our inconsistency.

We see a kind of physical integrity in an athlete, a musician, a dancer. They spend hours and hours of practice to discipline the movements of their bodies. We say, "She's a natural," because her moves seem instinctive, at one with her purpose. But, of course, the crucial integrity that shapes a person is integrity of heart, the integrity of persons who achieve the luminous success of living by their ideals. The pattern of their actions shapes and strengthens a power to act rightly that makes their behavior seem part of their very nature. But their behavior is not a given. It is a pattern established through clarity of commitment and consistency in choice.

Falling Short

But the best fall short. Failure need not be such as to destroy one's fundamental commitment. Experience teaches us to evaluate human action with care and nuance. Ordinarily a serious offense (e.g., taking the life of another) will engage a person's freedom more deeply and fully than a slight offense (e.g., an unkind word blurted out). In a particular situation, however, a certain deed, slight in itself, might carry weighty meaning because it engages our freedom quite fully and reflects a quite serious option. In evaluating an action we must weigh, together with the objective deed, the subjective intention and the degree to which the deed engages our freedom. Even in civil law, for example, we distinguish first-degree murder from manslaughter. Common sense also tells us to distinguish isolated acts from a pattern of activity that expresses and reinforces a fundamental option. We do not, for example, judge someone who on one or other occasion "overdoes it" to be an irresponsible lush. To evaluate a choice we have to consider the way choice reflects one's fundamental option and identity.

Still, even failure that does not destroy a basic commitment has consequences that require correction for the sake of integrity. Bad choices leave a residue of contradiction and confusion within us. When someone decides it is time to get over a bad mood, for example, it may be a while before a glum face is drawn into the new mood and spontaneously reflects good spirits in a ready smile. When a student does not perform adequately, a professor can grant a conditional pass. Though not altogether a failure, the student's academic act is not quite together, so the student has make-up work to do. Think of the process required, whatever the good will and determination, to adjust old habits to a new style of life, for example in marriage or in a foreign culture. When friends have a falling out, but then decide to get back together again, their first encounters are awkward. There remains a residue of their quarrel. The memory of hurt lingers and the ease of former times is missing. Their emotional and physical responses are not yet expressive of their desire for renewed friendship. It will take time to establish a unity in all the dimensions of their being so that there is no blush or stammering or hesitancy.

We also know the need to make amends when we have violated the trust of a friend. Of course, our willingness to make amends does not dictate what will be the response of our friend, for whose forgiveness we can only hope. But in some way we want to acknowledge, take responsibility for, and do something about our hurtful actions. There needs to be continuity in our story. We cannot simply detach our past like a trailer from a car. We cannot dismiss our previous life. The new person we want to be must grow out of the person we have been. We need to reconfigure ourselves in order to renew our friendship.

Purification

There are two aspects to the movement from dispersion to integrity, from failure to full reconciliation. Looking forward, thinking future, we see the movement positively, as a process of development and maturation. Looking backward, we see the movement negatively, as a process of reformation, which removes the consequences of failure and reshapes what was malformed. Reformation is in some degree disruptive, wrenching, painful. The pain is not a punishment arbitrarily imposed from without as a vindictive punishment, but something that arises from within, something built into the process of re-formation. We know this can represent quite a challenge. Think of a golfer's effort to "unlearn" a longstanding hitch in his swing or a smoker's struggle to overcome the power of an addiction.

The pain of reforming our lives, however, need not be seen as unrelieved suffering. When someone struggles to overcome an addiction, it is not just the goal that brings freedom and satisfaction. The process itself can become liberating, even exhilarating. Someone who undertakes to change out of love deals with the challenge much differently than someone on whom a change is imposed. For example, when in my selfishness I offend a friend, my continuing love stirs up the faith I have in my friend. My hope for reconciliation transfigures the pain involved in overcoming my selfishness. In addition, the reconciling love of my friend encourages me in my personal renewal.

The religious notion of purification makes sense, then, if we reflect on our own experience of failure, reform, and development toward integrity. In order to enter fully into the kingdom of God, we must attain the full ripening of our relationship with God. Whatever our fundamental option, our particular failures entail a lack of integration that does not simply disappear at death. There will need to be a transformation of the whole person, a process of maturation and integration that may be arduous and painful but will be happily embraced by someone in love.

Two points deserve emphasis. First, the essence of purgatory is purification and maturation, a perfecting of the person. The process is not a penalty arbitrarily imposed from without. The pain is the natural consequence of the lack of integrity and the need for reformation.

Second, love eases the pain in conversion and reform. If that is so in our reconciliation with one another, how much more in being reconciled with God, who "sent his only Son into the world, so that we might live through him" (1 John 4:9).

Purgatory should not be understood, therefore, in isolation, as a kind of mini-hell, a discrete phase of existence disengaged from the dynamism of faith and hope and love, detached from the process of transfiguration for union with God. Purification, maturation, integration: these are a movement in the Christian's dance of hope and faith and hope and love, a dance in which each of us moves within the whole communion of saints, led by the incalculably gracious Lord of the dance.

The Intermediate State

The Church teaches that a just person who dies prior to the consummation of history enjoys communion with God either immediately at death or upon completion of a process of purification. The soul, then, enjoys a heavenly existence even though not yet joined to its risen body. Traditional theology termed this period between death and the general resurrection an intermediate state.

The notion of an intermediate state provided an imaginative framework for situating the process of purification. It also supported a distinction between an individual's communion with God upon purification and the resurrection of the body at the end of history. But some problems connected with the notion of an intermediate state have led many theologians to abandon it.

The first problem involves the idea of there being a "state" between death and the Second Coming of Christ. Those who have died participate in the eternity of God. It seems wrong-headed,

therefore, to think of the dead as living in an interim period between death and the end of history.

What of purgatory, the purifying process by which individuals
are perfected in love? As we have seen, because we die into eternity, it makes sense to think of life beyond history in terms of
qualitative intensity rather than temporal duration. Consider a
simple example: if you hurt someone who is a close friend, you
go out of your way to avoid meeting that friend. It is just too
painful. And yet a meeting with that person might be something
very different. It might be a reconciling encounter. Suppose, after
a while, your friend invites you to dinner, an invitation that in effect says, "Let's think future."[1] In the course of the meal, the food,
the drink, and the conversation all help you to grow into your
friendship again. In the same way, a purifying maturation takes
place precisely in the encounter with the God of eternal life. We
can conceive purification, then, not as taking place in an intermediate state after death, but as a dimension of the process of dying:
we die into a purifying encounter with God.

A second problem with the notion of an intermediate state after
death concerns the idea of a soul living apart from its body. The
human person is a unity of spirit and matter. The soul is not an an-
gelic spirit, but the spirit of a human being, who is body as well
as soul. And so, it seems to make sense to affirm an immediate
resurrection of the whole being of a person who has died, transformed for immediate union with God in eternal life.[2]

Even when theology employed the notion of an intermediate
state between death and the general judgment, it was always
understood that the human soul somehow remained essentially
related to its body and thus to the physical world. Besides, to use
Paul's language, the spiritual body of a human person in eternal
life cannot be identified with the material body of life in history.
Indeed, even in history the human body is not a fixed quantity, but
is itself in constant process of change.

If, however, there is an immediate resurrection of the whole
person, what are we to think of the Church's constant practice of
prayer for the dead? The question puts into focus only one aspect
of a more fundamental question: How are we to understand the
efficacy of prayer?

Prayer for those who have gone before us marked with the sign of faith celebrates and reinforces the solidarity among God's people, the communion of saints. It is the same solidarity we express in our eucharistic liturgy when we speak of Christ who "pleads for us at the right hand of the Father" and of the saints "on whose constant intercession we rely for help." Living in hope, we entrust ourselves to the incalculable freedom of God. But God is the Father of our Lord Jesus Christ, who draws all of us together in one body because he shares the Spirit with us. We cannot think of ourselves, our development in history, our fulfillment in eternity, except in terms of a saving history we share. Our relationship with God touches, and is touched by, the relationship of all with God.

Hence, to pray for the departed means to pray in hope, commending them to the love of God. To attempt to say much more would be like trying to draw a diagram of how prayer works, a sort of theological circuitry chart like the one you find on the back of an electrical appliance. Insofar as our prayer for the dead is prayer for those already with God in eternity, it is prayer in solidarity. It is prayer in hope that the purification of the departed be suffused with love, and prayer for a glorious fulfillment that can only be complete when all God's people are perfected together at the end of time.

11

Hell

Hell is the condition of a person who is irretrievably alienated from God and whose eternity is, for that reason, a condition of torment. How can a Christian reconcile the notion of hell with faith in the God of forgiving love? Some cannot bring themselves to believe that God would impose eternal punishment on sinners. Others accept the teaching about hell but find it deeply threatening. Aware of their sinfulness, they live in fear and, perhaps, resentful anger at the very thought of hell. Others firmly believe in the merciful love of God, but the faith that sustains their hope inclines them to ask: Why does the victory of Christ over sin and death not silence all talk of hell?

Should we discard the notion of hell, or, as seems to be the case with many today, simply ignore it? The question is not speculative for Christians who want honestly to understand God and God's promise of eternal life. Can we imagine God leaving human persons in torment, utterly abandoned, without hope? Can any sinfulness on the part of a weak human creature warrant such punishment? We see punishment not as something vindictive, but as useful for reformation and rehabilitation. God's own word is that we should love our enemies. Are we to imagine God as implacably vengeful, beyond reconciliation? If not, why the threat of hell? Does the gospel mean to intimidate and coerce us? With the threat of hell hanging over us, how can we live in the joyful hope for which we pray in our liturgy?

Some Fathers of the Church, in fact, did not accept hell as a permanent state, arguing that mercy which is *divine* will ultimately restore all things in Christ.[1] But the Church continues to teach about hell and its eternity.[2] The Church, however, affirms only the possibility of hell. Whether anyone is actually living in this hellish condition must be left to the judgment of God.

The biblical teaching on hell is found in several passages which say that at the judgment every person will be called to account for their actions and will receive either reward or punishment in eternity. Matthew provides the most vivid description of the scene:

> When the Son of Man comes in his glory, and all the angels with him, then he will sit on his glorious throne. Before him will be gathered all the nations, and he will separate them one from another as a shepherd separates the sheep from the goats, and he will place the sheep at his right hand, but the goats at the left. Then the King will say to those at his right hand, "Come, O blessed of my Father, inherit the kingdom prepared for you from the foundation of the world." . . . Then he will say to those at his left hand, "Depart from me, you cursed, into the eternal fire prepared for the devil and his angels" (Matt 25:31-34, 41-42).

On the other hand, Scripture teaches that the reach of God's saving love is universal: "For God has consigned all men to disobedience, that he may have mercy upon all" (Rom 11:32).

In the following section we will try to clarify the notion of hell, weigh the possibility of hell, and reflect on the purpose of talk about hell.

The Religious Notion of Hell

Everyday experience can help us understand the religious notion of hell. We use the word to characterize all sorts of frustrating or painful experiences: a painful physical illness, loneliness or depression, arduous and demeaning conditions like poverty and political repression.

Let us focus on the misery that is most elemental, the loss of love. What is more painful than the loss of love? When we lose through death a child, a spouse, a parent, a friend, we know emptiness of heart. What is even worse is the loss of a loved one brought about by our own fault. That loss, more painful than emptiness, is a torment.

Strange as it may seem at first, there are times when we do create our own kind of hell. We reject love offered to us. We say, "I can get along without them." The irony is that we are saying, in effect, "To hell with *myself.*" What we reject we continue to need and yearn for at heart. To use a simple analogy, it is like turning away from friends and walking out on a party. We are not simply going elsewhere; we are going alone. But we continue to hear the laughter and music and we miss the company. No one imposed the estrangement on us. We chose it. Hell is a closing in on oneself, the self-inflicted pain of isolation and loneliness.

Unfortunately, we are able to lock ourselves into a pattern of self-enclosure, for our choices shape our vision, our way of seeing and thinking. In turn, our thinking can further constrict our imagination and so narrow our options. We see it in the stubbornness that becomes proud and defensive. We can make ourselves impervious to love, forgiveness, and reconciliation. What can friends do for us if we choose to repudiate them? Hence, the pain of loss continues. Our condition is hopeless.

When speaking of a definitive identity in eternity, we must be careful not to give the impression that heaven and hell are two possibilities of equal standing. That cannot be the case. Freedom is not a neutral capacity for choice that establishes indifferently this identity or that. Freedom has a *specific orientation:* our freedom is, in its structure, a reach to the God of self-giving love. Even if we choose what is bad, the choice is possible only because of a reach that is sustained and enabled by our relationship with God. To choose evil is contrary to the nature of freedom. Since a sinful decision runs counter to the orientation of freedom, it does not make sense to think that a decision for evil can define a person in the same depth as a decision for good, which expresses freedom authentically. Hence, to attribute to heaven and hell the same standing as possibilities would be to deny the fundamental dynamism at work in freedom.

There are, then, certain aspects of the notion of hell that fit our everyday experience. The *religious* notion, however, has two characteristics that make it acutely troublesome. First, it would mean losing what everyone most deeply yearns for at heart: personal union with God and with the whole of humankind redeemed by Christ. Second, hell would be misery without hope for recovery.

To weigh the possibility of hell we turn to the crux of the matter: freedom. We will consider, first, our freedom to reject God definitively, and then God's freedom not to leave someone in a condition of hopeless alienation.

Human Freedom and the Possibility of Hell

As we have seen, freedom aims at something complete and definitive. Through particular choices we opt for a basic style of being and define ourselves. The fruit of *becoming* through time is *being* in eternity.

We have already considered how we can fixate ourselves. As we reinforce an identity, we establish a mind-set/heart-set. The heart may become hardened even against God. Jesus once cured a man born blind. When the religious authorities opposed to Jesus challenged the man, he replied that this was the first time in the history of the world that anyone had opened the eyes of one born blind. His conclusion was: "If this man were not from God, he could do nothing" (John 9:33). But the authorities refused to listen and cast the man out. They thought of themselves as clearsighted but they had, in fact, shaped a mind-set/heart-set that blinded them to the truth about Jesus. The story of the blind man hits home. Try to challenge someone's basic convictions and commitments, in politics or religion, for example. They react with passion. Why? For the sake of some abstract theory? No, it is not just a mind-set that we challenge. We challenge their identity, who they have chosen to be at heart.

Of course, a full and final "no" to God would be self-destructive. God creates us precisely to share divine love. To reject God's

love, even though we are directed to it by the elemental dynamism of our hearts, would be to deny one's true self.

Why should there be such resistance to love? We resist giving
ourselves to what we cannot understand and control, but this is
not surprising. We have minds given us by God to think things
through and to make plans. It is natural to want understanding, if
we take that to mean intellectual control. We also have wills to express ourselves creatively and to manage our affairs. It is natural
to assert ourselves, to want to be in control. We want power and
by our God-given constitution have a right to it, power of mind
and power of will. The issue is: power for what? For Christians
the answer is unequivocal: power is to be put in the service of
love. And love means giving ourselves over to the freedom of another who is beyond our calculus and control. That is why we resist love. As the story of Adam and Eve has it, we want to gain
knowledge of good and evil, that is, the power to manipulate matters to our liking. We want things our way. We want to be like
God. And we end up alienated from others, the world, a shared
history. We are left with only ourselves, empty.

And so, the possibility of hell seems to make sense. To deny
this possibility would seem to trivialize our freedom, to imply
that we cannot define ourselves fully and finally before God. Hell
would be the consequence of human choice. It would be the
emptiness of irretrievable loneliness, hollowed out of me by my
own hand. For such a condition the image of fire serves well:
alienation, frustration, resentment, remorse, emptiness—all these
are like a fire that burns within us and consumes us.

Further, if we deny that hell is a possibility, what are we to say
about the wickedness at work in history and the manifold suffering it causes? In the face of sin-caused suffering, some cry out,
"There must be a hell." Can we talk about universal salvation
without trivializing the struggle between good and evil, without
minimizing the wickedness in our history?

However, the question about the possibility of hell is not pri-
marily about human freedom, but about God's freedom. We cannot set limits to God's gratuitous initiatives toward us.

Divine Freedom and the Possibility of Hell

God's own revelation tells us that God wills to save all humankind. In fact, God has already determined the thrust of human history. In Christ God has decisively inaugurated the kingdom. Christ's victory over sin and death would not be for us and for our salvation were it not to work its way in our history. In the context of the gospel as a whole, therefore, the *possibility* of hell cannot have the same status as the *reality* of heaven.

What of specific individuals? To dramatize personal accountability Jesus tells parables about stewardship and business acumen. But God did not create a cosmic business that sets human freedom in competition with the expertise and power of God. The creator, first of all, does not exist on the same level as a creature. God does not enter into competition with human persons. Rather, God establishes and sustains human freedom. Second, God creates human persons in order to share love. Human freedom works its way *within* the creative and self-giving love of God. God's power is love. God's expertise is compassion. Sin is not a costly miscalculation in a competitive business. Sin is a failure of love. Sin is a rejection of God's creative, self-giving love. But the love of God overcomes sin: "Where sin increased, grace abounded all the more, so that, as sin reigned in death, grace also might reign through righteousness to eternal life through Jesus Christ our Lord" (Rom 5:20-21).

Christ reveals a fundamental disparity between sin and God's superabundant grace. That disparity requires us to consider human freedom more fully, now in the context of divine freedom.

Given the disparity between decisions for good and evil, and, more importantly, the disparity between sin and the superabundant grace of God, perhaps we should qualify what was said earlier about human freedom as the capacity for self-definition. We need to address this question: "Is it really possible to imagine a human being utterly devoid of good, so completely evil that there is absolutely nothing for God to heal and fulfill in the resurrection?"[3]

To be sure, God creates and respects the human capacity for self-definition. But human freedom is sustained by God and, precisely as freedom, is subject to God's sovereign will. Christian faith has always taught that human freedom functions authentically only by the grace of God. God's grace does not compete with or undermine human freedom.[4] That is not an issue, of course, with one who freely accepts God, but neither should it be an issue in the case of someone who freely rejects God, insofar as that is possible. Given the inalienable openness to God at the heart of every human being, and given the inexhaustible love of God not as competing, but as sovereign, it seems possible to imagine the redemption even of someone who completely rejects God.

Perhaps we can make a distinction between a self-definition that is *total* and a self-definition that is *irreversibly final*.[5] Human beings by their structure have a specific goal. The goal is not a neutral eternity, any condition whatsoever that is irrevocable, but eternal life with God. As long as a person chooses to refuse God's love, even in a total self-definition, that person falls short of the final condition for which God created it. It would then follow that freedom can achieve an irreversibly final self-definition only in God.

Hope for Universal Salvation

Does a complete "no" on our part, insofar as that is conceivable, imply or demand a final "no" on God's part? The gospel proclaims God's radical compassion and solidarity with sinners. God's judgment is not simply an accounting procedure that records a person's condition at death. God's judgment establishes our eternity. Christ's resurrection demonstrates that in death the God of the living works a transformation and fulfillment of creation. Is it possible that we really do not have the last word about who we will become? Could it be that without violating human freedom the grace of God might "outwit" it?[6] That possibility— or, given the victory of Christ, that infinite probability—is not one that can be theoretically established, but one for which we can hope.

How might we imagine a reformation of one's fundamental option in or after death, since in death we move beyond history into eternity? Whatever the difficulty imagining eternal life, we ought not imagine it as a static, lifeless condition. Even in history we know of decisive commitments that define persons without freezing into a static frame the drama of love, the drama for which there is never enough time. If that is so in history, can we not conceive of change in a person who has not yet achieved fullness of life in eternity?

If an individual who *totally* rejects God does not do so *irretrievably*, then what was said earlier about someone undergoing purification could be applied to someone in a hellish condition. Like purgatory, hell would be understood as a condition that is not final, but still in process, the difference between the two being that a person being purified is already caught up irrevocably into union with God. In the process of movement through death to resurrection someone who had totally rejected God would remain in the condition of dying until there is purification and resurrection to fullness of life with God.

Of course, these notes on vitality after death and purification are only suggestive, but they realistically support our effort to imagine that those in a hellish state might be saved. The key points to keep in mind are the fundamental, inalienable orientation to God built into human nature and God's will to save everyone. Those points make plausible the restoration of all in Christ. If it is plausible, we can hope for it. For "with God all things are possible" (Matt 19:26).

Given the revelation of God as compassionate love, we *ought* to hope for the restoration of all in Christ. That is exactly what the Church does. The official prayer of the Church reflects its basic faith. According to a traditional saying, the rule of prayer is the rule of faith *(lex orandi, lex credendi)*. But since faith is the basis of hope, we might expand that to say the rule of prayer is the rule of hope *(lex orandi, lex sperandi)*. One example of the Church's prayer may serve as a fitting end to this discussion: "Lord, accept the offering of your Church; and may what each individual offers up to the honor of your name lead to the salvation of all. For this we pray to you through Christ our Lord."[7] Christian faith encourages us and Christian love impels us to hope for the salvation of all.

12

Hope in History

Finally, it is time to bring all of our considerations together and focus them on the life we are living at the present time. For us, to live in the present means to make a future in this world. What does Christian hope mean for our future in this world?

The Question

As we have seen, the Gospels maintain a tension between present and future. On the one hand, the reign of God is a *future* reality: the kingdom will be fully established only at the end of time. On the other hand, the reign of God is a *present* reality: God has already inaugurated the reign in Christ. Christian life involves both hope for fullness of life beyond history and hope for a meaningful life within history. The tension between the two raises the question of the meaning of human accomplishment within history.

The question about hope in history bears both on our efforts to accomplish something in history and on what we might accomplish by our efforts. Since the reign of God is God's gift, what is the use of all our present labor? Since our future is eternal life, how can we be confident that what we accomplish here makes any difference in the long run?[1]

Thus, we come to the age-old, hill-of-beans question: Does our work for a future in this world amount to anything more than a hill of beans? How should Christians imagine life in the world before death? Is life now simply a trial that we must endure until God provides release? Is the world a stage where we can perform acts of virtue, but in a drama whose scenes have no enduring significance? Should we hunker down, quietly resigned to make the best of it, or can we hope to shape a future within history that will embody the vision of Christ?

We need to address this question: What is the relationship between the life we make in the world and eternal life?

A Historical Note

A detailed review of Christian attitudes toward history in the world lies beyond the scope of this book. Nonetheless, it might be helpful to note some important moments.

Responsibility for one another stands at the center of the revelation about the kingdom of God. Israel understood itself as a people. Salvation did not mean salvation of individual souls, but of a nation—or, as they came to realize, of a community of nations. The prophets focused on the way people lived together in society, repeatedly chastising them for social injustices. Jesus summed up the Law and the prophets with a twofold command that joined love of God with love of one's neighbor. In turn, the early Christian community understood Christian life as essentially communal, a building up of the body of Christ. Sin was understood to harm the entire community. As a result, penance was very much a public matter, reconciliation with God through reconciliation with the community. The cause of God is the cause of humankind, victorious only in social solidarity.

The tension between concern for human solidarity and the shape of society on the one hand, and, on the other, concern for the things that are above, inevitably gave rise to different emphases in the way Christians imagined responsibility for life in the world. When Constantine made Christianity the official religion of his empire, questions about the relationship between the life of faith and the political order, between Church and state, came to the fore. Theologians (like Augustine in his *City of God*) consistently labored to interpret the direction and meaning of history in relation to eternal life. With the development of monasticism came an emphasis on the spiritual perfecting of the individual soul, and a kind of individualism worked its way into Christian spirituality.

The rise of humanism by highlighting human freedom and the beauty of human creativity focused attention on the works of humankind. Religious controversies from the time of the Reformation onward exposed once more the tension between concern for human accomplishment in history and reliance on God. How are we to understand the relationship between human nature and divine grace, between human freedom and divine omnipotence? How should we envision human efforts and evaluate human accomplishments in the world? These controversies have defined the possibilities Christians may hope for in our world as well as the responsibility Christians feel for shaping a future within history.

In the modern period developments in empirical and social science, as well as in technology and economic structures, gave new form to questions about hope in history. During this period some political and economic philosophies developed a highly individualistic notion of human freedom. But other systems of thought expressed a dramatically heightened sense of historical process and the power of social structures. We do not live in a history that is a given. Rather, we live by making a history. We live by creating the social structures that shape our life together. These social structures powerfully influence patterns of behavior. More fundamentally, they prejudice the way we understand ourselves and our world, and the way we imagine our future together. Reflection on human existence as a historical and social process gave rise in some schools of thought to enduring criticism of Christian faith.

Critique of Christian Hope

Critics claim that Christian hope for eternal life alienates us from our world and our work by making them insignificant. Hope for fulfillment beyond history removes the incentive to work toward a society of justice and peace within history. The conviction that the kingdom is God's gift enervates our creativity and sense

of responsibility for our future in the world. We ought to rid ourselves of childish dependence on God. We should assume responsibility for shaping a humane future in the world and
cultivate the human ingenuity and creativity that bring progress.

That critique, well known since the time of Marx and Freud,
has this merit: genuine concern for a humane future in the world
motivates us to work toward a future when justice and peace will
be the rule.[2] Indeed, it was a dialogue between Marxist philosophers and Christian theologians that gave impetus to contemporary reflection on Christian hope.

The practice of Christian faith has sometimes given warrant for
the critique just outlined. Some Christians have thought it an act
of piety to set the glory of God over against human achievement.
They intended to reverence the power and graciousness of God by
denigrating what is human. Sometimes, too, Christians have held
that acceptance of the status quo in economic and political life
was a religious duty that will be rewarded in heaven. They have,
in effect, exploited the promise of eternal life to ignore the demands of social justice.

Does Christian hope support indifference to social justice and
discourage efforts to shape a humane future in the world? Or does
it impel a commitment to the humanization of the world? If so,
how do we integrate hope for the historical future and hope for
eternal life? And so, we ask the question one more time: What is
the relationship between a future we work for in history and eternal life?

The Second Vatican Council

Whatever the pendulum swings in focus and style, the Church
has never turned from responsibility for the world. Over the cen-
turies the Church has addressed complex social problems, refin-
ing its judgment about such matters as international law, usury,
and slavery. The Church, itself a major factor in political developments within and between nations, needed continually to sort
out its proper role in public affairs.

Developments in the modern period, however, brought a dramatically new consciousness of the historical nature of human

existence and the importance of social structures in human development. Beginning with Pope Leo XIII's The Condition of Labor (1891), the Church has elaborated a significant body of social teaching through a series of papal encyclicals, addresses, and apostolic letters. The present generation has also witnessed a remarkable succession of such documents, beginning in 1961 with Pope John XXIII (Christianity and Social Progress and Peace on Earth), continuing with Pope Paul VI (On the Development of Peoples, The Eightieth Anniversary of "Rerum Novarum"), and recently Pope John Paul II (On Human Work and The Social Concern of the Church).[3] Complementing those and other important declarations, the bishops of the United States have issued, among other statements, two lengthy pastoral letters: The Challenge of Peace and Economic Justice for All. That steady effort emphatically expresses Christian hope in history.

One document of the Vatican Council II stands at the center of contemporary Church teaching, due to its originality, its foundational quality, and its authority: Pastoral Constitution on the Church in the Modern World *(Gaudium et spes)*.[4] The constitution tells how the Church, to be its authentic self, must understand our world, learn from it, critique its development, and serve its progress. The opening lines detail the Church's concern exquisitely: "The joys and the hopes, the griefs and the anxieties of the men of this age, especially those who are poor or in any way afflicted, these too are the joys and the hopes, the griefs and the anxieties of the followers of Christ" (1).

To describe how they are approaching their task the council fathers employ a phrase made popular by John XXIII, saying it is their duty to read "the signs of the times" (Matt 16:3):

> The Church seeks but a solitary goal: to carry forward the work of Christ Himself under the lead of the befriending Spirit. And Christ entered this world to give witness to the truth, to rescue and not to sit in judgment, to serve and not to be served.
>
> To carry out such a task, the Church has always had the duty of scrutinizing the signs of the times and of interpreting them in the light of the gospel. . . . We must therefore recognize and understand the world in which we live, its expectations, its longings, and its often dramatic characteristics (3–4).

Part I delineates the Church's vision of the world.[5] It treats the dignity of the human person, the community of humankind, the meaning of human activity in the world, and the role of the Church in the modern world. It criticizes an individualistic ethics and emphasizes the communitarian nature of the person. We are called to recognize the interdependence of the person and society, promote the common good, and work for social justice.

The Meaning of Human Activity

The Pastoral Constitution addresses the issue of hope in history directly: "Through his labors and his native endowments man has ceaselessly striven to better his life. . . . What is the meaning and value of this feverish activity? . . . To the achievement of what goal are the strivings of individuals and societies heading?" (33).

What the Constitution teaches about the meaning of human activity comprises four basic points.

First, contrary to what critics assert, hope in God does not diminish human freedom to create a future in history. Human and divine freedom are not in competition. God creates our freedom. Since we depend on God precisely for our freedom, we are not more free the less we depend on God. Further, our relation to God defines and summons us at heart, so nearness to God fulfills, rather than compromises, our individuality. Hence, our relationship with God does not entrap or diminish us; rather, it liberates us. Because of our hope in God, whose resources utterly transcend our own, our own limitations do not trap us. Hope in God gives us the security and strength for authentic freedom. Indeed, as with Jesus, even our apparent failure can lead to an ultimate victory. The constitution declares that the triumphs of humanity are a sign of the greatness of God who empowers human freedom (34).

Second, hope in eternal life does not diminish our responsibility for the world; rather, it mandates care for our world. God created and sustains the world out of love. God wills, therefore, that we respect the structures and laws of the created world. So, too, we must respect the methods and achievements proper to science and the arts through which we come to understand and develop our world. Hope for eternal life should stimulate efforts to create a better world. What decisively reveals the value of human accomplishment is God's will to perfect it in eternal life. We must measure the value of human accomplishment within history by the creative, redemptive love of God.

Third, we do not know specifically how the world we shape in history will be transformed in eternal life. The heart of history is a dramatic dialogue with God. We must relate to God in hope, not because of God's indifference, but because of the incalculable creativity of God, who will bring the world to fulfillment in a kingdom beyond history. Revelation has taught us the plot lines of the drama: while the shape of the world as disfigured by sin will pass away, the blessedness of fulfillment will surpass the longings of the human heart.

Finally, the connection between what we accomplish in history and the kingdom of God is this: the kingdom is already present in mystery. God is at work in us through the Spirit in a way we cannot calculate. Because of God's empowering love our work contributes to the realization of the divine plan for history.

To describe how our cultivation of this earth contributes to the divine design the constitution states that earthly progress is able to give some kind of *foreshadowing* of the kingdom. The metaphor serves well: it indicates an anticipation of future perfection, while connoting that the kingdom is present now in mystery.

The constitution designates the purpose that should guide our striving: to serve one another by bringing earthly resources to the service of human life, by nurturing human dignity and solidarity, by shouldering, like Christ, the cross for justice and peace. This goal should be the object of our activity: the construction of a better world, a better ordering of human society. Each of us can contribute to our enterprise in accordance with our diverse gifts. Through our work in the world we develop ourselves and move beyond our individual selves. Greater than technological advances and material riches is the establishment of justice in social relationships (38).

Two final points may be especially helpful for understanding how Christian hope works in history. First, if we place our trust in the design of the creator, we will come to recognize that human progress can serve our true happiness (37). Second, the Spirit of

Christ not only arouses in our hearts a desire for the age to come, but by that very fact animates and strengthens our present efforts to make life more human and to render the earth more submissive to this goal (38). The constitution thus links trust in the design of the creator with appreciation for human progress; it links desire for the age to come with effort to make life more humane. Trust in God's plan, life in the Spirit: that is a way of life, not a theory. Perhaps it is only in actually shaping a more humane world that we will acquire insight into how Christian hope works in history. The insight does not come through logic but from a felt experience. In the act of working toward a more humane future we feel both the enduring value of our work and a desire for its fulfillment. As a popular expression has it: "In the doing is the knowing." Those who do the works of love come to such an understanding.

Do those indications of the constitution adequately spell out the connection between what we accomplish in history and the shape of our ultimate fulfillment? What is the key to the mystery by which the kingdom is present, by which we contribute now to God's mysterious design? The key is not a tidy formula. The key is the dynamic of love. The constitution puts it clearly: the basic law of human perfection, and so of the world's transformation, is love.

Love does not wait for a blueprint, complete in every detail. That basic fact becomes clear if we consider the example of parents. Love for their children impels them to think future. Now a real future means hoping, for hoping impels us to imagine possibilities. Parents imagine possibilities for their children. Otherwise, they cannot commit themselves to work for their children's future. They cannot predict in detail the future for which they work. Even so, they must commit themselves in hope. Love must work its way. They will be hopeful because they believe that their love will yield fruit that will endure.

One particular parent stands out for me as an example of this sort of hope. I knew a woman years ago who was in the maternity ward waiting to deliver her eighth child. She had seven others at home, the oldest of whom was nine. Five months earlier, her husband had died of injuries sustained in an auto accident. She got

up and walked over to look out the window. With some appre-
hension a nurse quickly moved to stand by her side. The woman
laughed when she told me the story. She said, "I understood the
nurse's concern, but I thought, 'Are you kidding me? The thought
of jumping out a fifth-story window would never enter my
mind.'" This was a woman whose hope was sustained by a profound faith in God. Her love for all her children impelled her to
look to the future with hope.

We have come full circle: the dance of hope and faith and hope
and love and hope. The drama with real hope for a future is a
drama in which love works its way in hope, based on faith. Love
gives our hope direction and strength. By doing the works of love
we respond effectively to anyone who calls us to account for the
hope that is in us (1 Pet 3:15).

Suggestions
for Further Reading

Balthasar, Hans Urs von. *Dare We Hope "That All Men Be Saved"?* San Francisco: Ignatius Press, 1988.

Becker, Ernest. *The Denial of Death.* New York: The Free Press, 1973.

Daley, Brian. *The Hope of the Early Church: A Handbook of Christian Eschatology.* New York: Cambridge University Press, 1991.

Lynch, William F. *Images of Hope: Imagination as Healer of the Hopeless.* Baltimore: Helicon, 1965.

Miller, Jerome A. *The Way of Suffering.* Washington, D.C.: Georgetown University Press, 1986.

O'Brien, D. J., and Thomas A. Shannon. *Renewing the Earth: Catholic Documents on Peace, Justice and Liberation.* Garden City, N.J.: Image Books, 1977.

Phan, Peter C. *Eternity in Time: A Study of Karl Rahner's Eschatology.* Cranbury, N.J.: Associated University Presses, 1988.

Endnotes

Introduction

[1]For a lucid summary of traditional Church teaching on eschatology see the recently issued *Catechism of the Catholic Church* (Mahwah, N.J.: Paulist Press, 1994) 258–75.

Chapter 1

[1]I am indebted especially to two authors: William F. Lynch, *Images of Hope* (Baltimore: Helicon, 1965), and Karl Rahner, "The Theology of Hope," *Theological Investigations* 10, trans. David Bourke (New York: Seabury Press, 1977) 66–86.

[2]For this reason, when we speak of a disposition that governs a person's behavior, we should refer to it not simply as a mind-set, but as a mind-set/heart-set. Otherwise the expression obscures a person's responsibility in adopting this particular disposition.

Chapter 3

[1]This paragraph and the one preceding I have taken from my essay, "Anticipating Jesus Christ: An Account of Our Hope," *A World of Grace,* ed. Leo J. O'Donovan (New York: Seabury Press, 1980) 107–19.

[2]John Courtney Murray, *The Problem of God* (New Haven, Conn.: Yale University Press, 1964) 104.

Chapter 4

[1]The expression "kingdom of God" appears in the New Testament more than 150 times (Matthew uses "kingdom of Heaven," a Jewish circumlocution). The original Greek term might be better translated as "reign," which suggests the active exercise of sovereignty, since "king-

dom" suggests a static place or realm. On the other hand, since God's reign has not yet reached its definitive fulfillment, there is merit in using "kingdom" when referring to a reign that is fully achieved. To retain the merits in each translation I employ both.

[2]Donald Senior, "Reign of God," *The New Dictionary of Theology,* ed. Joseph A. Komonchak and others (Wilmington, Del.: Michael Glazier, 1987) 860.

Chapter 5

[1]Zachary Hayes, *Visions of a Future* (Wilmington, Del.: Michael Glazier, 1989) 191.

Chapter 6

[1]From early on, theologians speculated in detail about the glorified body. Medieval theology attributed four properties to the bodies of the just: impassability (no suffering), subtlety ("spiritualization"), agility (ease and speed of movement), and clarity (radiant beauty). These properties, it was argued, follow from the complete dominion of the soul over the glorified body.

[2]See John R. Sachs, *The Christian Vision of Humanity* (Collegeville: The Liturgical Press, 1991) 98: "In one sense heaven is *God;* heaven is the self-communication of God's own life to the human world through Jesus Christ. In another sense, we may say that heaven is the *world* brought to its final glory in and by God's saving love."

Chapter 7

[1]Pastoral Constitution on the Church in the Modern World *(Gaudium et spes),* no. 18. The translation is from Walter M. Abbott, ed., *The Documents of Vatican II* (New York: America Press, 1966).

[2]Ibid.

[3]Decree for the Greeks, Council of Florence (1439). The text may be found in J. Neuner and J. Dupuis, eds., *The Christian Faith in the Doctrinal Documents of the Catholic Church* (New York: Alba House, 1982) 686.

[4]Decree on Original Sin, Council of Trent (1546). See *The Christian Faith in the Doctrinal Documents of the Catholic Church,* 137–8.

[5]Karl Rahner, *On the Theology of Death* (New York: Herder and Herder, 1961) 41.

[6]Ibid., 34–35.

Chapter 8

[1]If one does not believe in miracles, faith in the resurrection is ruled out from the start. Of course, it will be crucial to notice how one defines a miracle: as an adventitious intrusion of God into the development of human nature, or as an act of God that brings to fulfillment and reveals the deepest potential of human nature as ordered, graciously, to the life of God.

Chapter 9

[1]Empirical science can in some sense stand above the objects it studies. It can investigate the dynamics of what goes on *in the world.* Since God, however, is not a being among the beings in the world, divine causality can never become an object of empirical science.

[2]Zachary Hayes, *Visions of a Future* (Wilmington, Del.: Michael Glazier, 1989) 202.

Chapter 10

[1]This future orientation needs to be always present in celebrating the eucharistic meal, which is itself an anticipation of the messianic banquet in the kingdom of God.

[2]The most recent official teaching of the Church does not exclude the possibility of an immediate resurrection of the whole person. See Peter C. Phan, *Eternity in Time* (Cranbury, N.J.: Associated University Presses, 1988) 133.

Chapter 11

[1]John R. Sachs, "Apocatastasis in Patristic Theology," *Theological Studies* 54 (1993) 617–40.

[2]*The Catechism of the Catholic Church* (Mahwah, N.J.: Paulist Press, 1994) no. 1035.

[3]John R. Sachs, "Current Eschatology: Universal Salvation and the Problem of Hell," *Theological Studies* 52 (1991) 237, n. 40.

[4]Think of love between human persons. When under the influence of the gracious love of another, we experience our freedom not as constricted by that love, but liberated and fulfilled.

[5]Sachs, "Current Eschatology," 246ff.

[6]The notion comes from Edith Stein. See Sachs, "Current Eschatology," 246.

[7]Prayer over the Gifts, Twenty-Fourth Week in Ordinary Time.

Chapter 12

[1]The reality of evil and suffering in our history gives poignant intensity to the question of whether, in view of death and resurrection, all human effort and accomplishment is as straw.

[2]The critique finds reinforcement in any philosophy that identifies true knowing only with what we can establish through sense experience or science, and acknowledges no mystery to existence other than what science has not yet figured out.

[3]These citations do not exhaust the list.

[4]Walter M. Abbott, ed., *The Documents of Vatican II* (New York: The America Press, 1966). References to the text are by paragraph numbers.

[5]Part II addresses specific dimensions of life in the world: marriage and the family; the development of culture; economic and social life; political life; and the community of nations.